The HMO Expert

Master the strategy to multiply your income

Richard Leonard

First published in 2025 by Richard Leonard Publishing

ISBN 978-1-9193731-0-2

Edited by Sarah Walker

A CIP catalogue record for this book is available from the British Library.

Printed and bound by IngramSpark.

Cover design by Yasir Nadeem

Typesetting by Sarah Walker

The HMO Expert

Master the strategy to multiply your income

The definitive guide to HMO success for modern property entrepreneurs.

Richard Leonard

Dedication

This book is dedicated to my son, William John Leonard, who inspires me every single day. You are my greatest motivation, and everything I do is with you in mind.

To my amazing wife Kathrine and our wonderful family—Alex, Chris, James, Kate, and Smalls—thank you for being my rock, my support, and my reason to keep going, even on the hardest days. I love you all more than words can say.

A very special mention goes to my Mum and Dad, Dorren and Bill, who believed in me from the very beginning. They were my first ever investors, and without their love, trust, and support, none of this would have been possible.

This book is a result of all the encouragement, sacrifice, and belief from those closest to me. I am forever grateful.

Thank you, from the bottom of my heart.

Contents

Watching you bring this book to life has been such a beautiful part of our journey together. I've seen the dedication, the late nights, the quiet doubts, and the unwavering determination that's carried you through — I am so proud of you.

This book is more than just words on a page — it reflects everything we've built together, not only in life but in our property journey. Every decision, every challenge, every step forward has been shaped by the love, support, and partnership we've shared along the way.

Working side by side as a team, through all the highs and lows, has been one of the greatest gifts — and I'm so grateful for what we continue to build together. Our loving family, our work, and our dreams are all part of this story.

With all my love, always.

Your wife, Kathrine

Introduction

So, you'd like to invest in HMOs. Excellent decision! HMOs (Houses in Multiple Occupation) have been among the most lucrative UK property investments over the last two decades.

The government defines a property as an HMO if at least three tenants live there, forming more than one household, and toilet, bathroom or kitchen facilities are shared with other tenants. If there are five or more occupants under those conditions, it's a 'large HMO'.

More individual tenants means more rental income, which results in a much better gross yield than if you let the same property to a single family. And if you're doing it right, your net yield and profits should be significantly higher as well.

But HMO investment is about far more than buying a property and filling it with tenants. It's a serious business undertaking, and it requires know-how, planning and elbow grease. As with any business, there are a whole load of potential pitfalls, and getting any of them wrong could put a serious dent in your finances.

To be a successful HMO landlord, you need to provide comfortable, safe, legally compliant, well-managed accommodation that appeals to your specific tenant market - and that can be very hard work, particularly in the early days.

The good news is that with the right approach and attitude, the reward is 100% worth it.

My aim with this book is to give you a straightforward introduction to HMO investing and illustrate how you can build a profitable portfolio with minimal stress. It's a step-by-step guide that takes you through each stage of the process, from choosing the right location and property, refurbishing and getting it ready to rent, to managing tenants and your investment into the future.

My own particular strength (and favourite part of the business) is renovation and refurbishment. I love the challenge of taking a basic property and turning it into the best and most profitable version of itself – somewhere tenants happily choose to live. Happy tenants equal a lower turnover of rooms, minimal hassle and more secure profits. So I'll be talking you through everything from the design and planning of the property to the addition of essential amenities and how you can really make your HMO stand out in this competitive business.

(My first book, 'HMO Property Renovation & Refurbishment Success', which I co-wrote with fellow investor, Nick Fox, goes into this stage in much more detail - you can buy it now on Amazon.)

Over the past 20 years, I've learned exactly what does (and doesn't) work with HMOs, and now I'm passing on my experience, lessons, and methods in what I hope is an engaging and inspiring read. Property investment should never be dull, and I've included lots of real-life examples and anecdotes to encourage you that, even though it's a serious commitment, being an HMO landlord is also fun - and hugely rewarding.

Whether your goal is to build a long-term property portfolio that will enable you to exit the 9-to-5, or simply to earn some additional income, the HMO model can help you achieve it. With the right guidance and a willingness to learn, you can set yourself up for prosperity in one of the UK's most vibrant property strategies.

Right, grab yourself a cuppa (or something stronger) and let's get underway!

Note: The national legislation for HMOs and local authority rules around planning and licensing that I talk about in this book relate to England. If you're based in any other part of the UK, check your own government and council websites, as there will be some differences.

RENTED
01438 861280

Chapter One

Why Invest in HMO Property?

There's no denying that HMOs are more time-consuming to manage and cost more to run than other types of property rental. They're also more heavily regulated and often require more capital input at the outset for renovation, refurbishment and furnishing.

Sounding good yet?!

Okay, those are challenges, but don't worry, they're all surmountable and I'll talk you through them in the coming chapters. For now, I want to focus on the huge benefits of investing in HMOs, which – as thousands of landlords would agree – greatly outweigh the negatives.

Market-beating rental income and profit

If you're looking for regular income, few property investment strategies offer the same level of month-on-month profit potential.

Unlike traditional buy-to-let, where you have a single household renting the whole property, HMO landlords let individual bedroom units on separate tenancy agreements. More tenants means multiple rents that can give you two to three times the income you'd get from letting the property to one household. That results in a higher yield and better cash flow.

Let's take a closer look at the income potential:

A typical three-bedroom home might rent for £1,200 a month as a single let. However, if you could convert the same property to a five-bedroom HMO and let each room for £600 a month (bills included), your rental income would shoot up to £3,000. Even with increased management, maintenance and utility costs, the opportunity to massively boost your profit margin is clear.

As far as my own portfolio is concerned, our six-bedroom properties here in the South-East of England each generate a net (pre-tax) monthly profit of between £1,500 and £2,000 per calendar month. That's every property, every month!

A more stable, lower-risk investment

With a standard single-let rental, there's always the risk of a void period between tenancies, where the property is empty and you don't have any rent coming in. Meanwhile, you've still got costs to cover – mortgage, maintenance, etc. – which you'll have to subsidise until you get a new tenant.

But with an HMO, even if one tenant leaves and the room is unoccupied for a short while, you've still got the income from all the other tenants. If you've done your sums and invested wisely, around 50% of the rental income should cover all the property-related expenditure and the rest is profit. So, if you've got a five-bedroom HMO, even with two empty rooms your investment should still be self-funding. (And we never have two empty rooms!!)

This income stability, combined with the on-going rental profit potential, is the biggest reason landlords choose the HMO strategy. But it's supported by a number of other benefits that make it a sound long-term investment prospect.

High demand

The cornerstone of any buy-to-let investment is ensuring there is strong demand for the type of property you're letting. And there's no question that room rentals within a shared house are in consistently high demand in towns and cities all across the UK.

The majority of HMO tenants are students, young professionals, key workers and both UK and non-UK nationals in lower-paid jobs, and there are three big reasons they're in the market for this kind of accommodation:

1. **Affordability.** With the price of home ownership and whole-property rental simply unaffordable for many people, all-inclusive room rentals are a much more cost-effective option, and the fixed monthly price makes it easier to budget.

   As the cost-of-living crisis rolls on, we're seeing more tenants than ever actively seeking cheaper accommodation options, particularly in urban industrial & high-tech areas, where there's steady demand from young professionals relocating for work.

   London, Manchester, and Birmingham are just three of the major metropolitan areas where there's a growing need for HMOs. Most of the employees in these areas can't afford single occupancy apartments, so high-quality HMOs offer the perfect solution.

2. **Convenience.** HMOs give tenants their own private room and then shared access to all the amenities of a larger family home. For a relatively low cost, they can live in good quality accommodation in a town or city centre and enjoy easy access to public transport, retail and leisure facilities.

3. **Community.** Shared housing gives people – particularly those who may have just moved to the area or are starting a new job or study course – an instant 'family' environment. The most successful HMOs have a decent communal area where tenants can socialise (e.g. a

spacious dining kitchen) and we find many of our tenants form strong friendships with their housemates.

So, if you can offer a good standard of living in a location with high employment opportunities and/or universities/colleges and excellent transport links, HMOs can be the most rewarding type of property investment, out-stripping normal buy-to-lets in levels of demand and occupancy.

As at Q4 2025, we have no voids across 350 rooms and tenant waiting lists are the norm!

Opportunity to add value

Of course, you can add capital value to many types of property through renovation, extension and conversion, but when it comes to buy to let, the HMO strategy gives you a real incentive.

With a single household let, there's usually very little immediate financial benefit to adding rooms. If you've got a two or three-bedroom home that you want to rent out to a family, they're not going to pay much more rent simply because there's a spare bedroom or an extra study – so why would you bother spending money on converting a loft or building an extension?

But with HMOs, every additional room that you can let as a single unit is hundreds more pounds in your pocket every month, so it makes sense to buy a property with potential. Providing you make sure you're adding appropriate, meaningful space, that should also boost the capital value and increase your equity – ideally by more than it cost you to do the work!

The more equity you have, the more refinancing options become available to you, and that can help increase your return on investment (ROI).

Even creative changes in layout, such as removing internal walls to create a spacious communal area or turning 'wasted' recesses into en-suite shower rooms, can help attract higher-quality tenants who are willing to pay a premium.

The caveat is that increasing income and returns in this way relies on carrying out careful research before you commit to buying, to make sure the figures stack up. More detail on this in Chapters 3 and 6.

Chapter Summary

If you're trying to decide between investing in a 'traditional' buy to let and an HMO, here's a handy summary of the pros & cons of high-quality HMOs versus single lets:

The downsides

- A specialist HMO mortgage is required, which means a smaller pool of lenders and potentially a more expensive product

- Usually higher start-up costs for getting ready to rent

- More planning, licensing and health & safety governance – additional legislation to know and comply with

- More time-consuming and costly - both in terms of property maintenance and management of multiple individual tenants/tenancies

BUT....

The upsides

✓ Can generate 2-3 times the rental income and net profit (with 5-6 lettable rooms)

✓ Average UK yield across all HMOs is 10.4%, versus 7% for the buy-to-let market as a whole (Q4 2024) *(lendlord.io & ukfinance.org.uk)*

✓ Multiple separate rent payments virtually wipe out the risk of voids

✓ Consistent, high demand from a wide variety of tenants

- ✓ Investment in adding rooms generates immediate income
- ✓ Stable long-term investment

Sure, single lets are easier, but once you've got your head (and business) around what goes into creating a quality HMO, and you start to see the monthly profits roll in, there's every chance that you'll be hooked. I certainly am!

Chapter Two

The HMO Mindset

Before we move on to the nuts and bolts of the HMO strategy from a practical perspective, I want to talk about the kind of mindset you need to succeed in this business.

Simply running the numbers and buying what stacks up on paper as the right property won't necessarily lead to a successful investment.

HMOs are not vanilla buy-to-let properties. You need to manage them actively, keep up with the (many) regulations and maintain good relationships with your tenants. That means rolling your sleeves up and being a hands-on landlord, accepting that maintenance issues, tenant turnover, queries and complaints might test your patience. But, with the right attitude, every hurdle becomes just another opportunity to refine your business model.

The best HMO landlords take a holistic approach. Their properties form part of their wider long-term financial and lifestyle goals and they are well prepared to evolve and adapt their business according to changes in the market – and changes in their own circumstances. They understand there will always be challenges to overcome and problems that need solving, and they're happy to step up and tackle them.

An Entrepreneurial Spirit

Entrepreneurs are always looking for new things. New ideas, new income streams, new projects, new solutions, better ways of doing anything and everything.

Is that you?

If so, you'll probably relish the challenge of HMOs and delight in the opportunity to craft your own version of this highly profitable investment vehicle. I'll give you enough of the nuts and bolts to get you started, but then you'll need that drive to keep tweaking, refining and improving your business as you go in order to keep your income and profits up.

Even as a child, I wanted to make my own money. I started off with paper rounds before school, then moved on to washing cars for 50p a go. It began with just the neighbours in my street, but word spread around the whole estate and, before long, I had to rope in my brother and a few friends just to keep up with demand. We even threw in a bit of dog walking for extra cash!

I still remember that old Holborn tobacco tin, rattling with coins every Sunday evening as I collected payments. I always looked after my team and took the business seriously, making sure we reinvested in proper sponges and fresh leathers. And that's the property business in a nutshell: if you want to be successful, look after your people and always reinvest a portion of your profits.

Eventually, an opportunity came up at the local pub. I was too young to work behind the bar, so I became the cellar boy instead. And that's where I first truly learned the value of working hard - and saving even harder.

Entrepreneurs also think in about building wealth in a different way to most people. Employees plan to work their way up the ladder, getting a better salary with every promotion and, as their income rises, they might invest more and more in various financial assets – but they're still trading their time for money. And as their role within a company becomes more significant over the years, the number of hours they have to personally invest in that company increases.

In contrast, all the entrepreneurs I know are focused on creating passive income streams. That's where the money rolls in every day, whether they're personally working in the business or not. Sure, they have to put in long hours for the first few years to get ventures off the ground but, from the word go, they're thinking about what structures, systems, processes and people they need to put in place so that the business will run without them and they no longer have to trade their time for money.

Ironically, because the entrepreneurial mind is always looking for the next challenge and the next opportunity to succeed, the time they free up for themselves with one venture is usually immediately ploughed into the next! But by setting up multiple passive revenue streams, they are gaining two incredibly important things: time freedom and freedom of choice.

That means, although they love to work, they're not forced to so something they don't enjoy just because there are bills to pay. Because they have time and a level of financial security, they have the freedom to choose something that really interests them. And if they want a holiday and to spend time with loved ones, they can just do it.

My HMO portfolio ticks along brilliantly without me. That's not to say I don't work on it – I do – but it's not a daily or even weekly requirement. So I recently spent three weeks travelling in Europe with my family, and when I came home, it wasn't back to the grindstone in an office, I went off to look at some new development opportunities and catch up with a couple of fellow investors.

I could just keep an eye on my portfolio and spend a lot of time sitting in the garden – my HMO business is highly profitable. But that wouldn't fulfil me, and if you've got the kind of entrepreneurial flair that will enable you to build your own property business, it wouldn't fulfil you either.

Thinking Like an Investor

Hard work and entrepreneurial flair are two of the key pillars that will support your HMO business, but a third is the ability to view property as an investment vehicle; to treat it as a business asset and take emotion out of the equation. Most of the emotion, anyway.

Just a little side-bar… I've heard countless property investment 'gurus' telling people that when they're buying a rental, they need to remember it's not a home for themselves, it's a business, so it doesn't matter whether they like the look of it – it's simply about whether it stacks up as a good financial deal. I don't agree.

Of course it's got to stack up, but while it might not be *your* home, it's home to your tenants. And when you come to sell, 15 or 20 years down the line, some prospective buyers are going to be looking for a home. So, before you even take the time to do the figures on a potential purchase, just step back and think about whether your gut likes the bricks and mortar. Because if it's not visually appealing in some way, no matter how good the numbers are on paper, in my opinion you're adding risk.

Back to the business mindset. Successful HMO investors make informed decisions based on facts, figures, and proven methods. They take time to analyse market data and trends, and consider how they can minimise costs and risks to maximise ongoing profits and create long-term wealth for themselves.

As an investment, HMOs are a double-strander, with both short-term and long-term gains to be had. On the one hand, you've got to keep rents as high as reasonably possible and ongoing expenditure in check to ensure decent monthly cashflow and profits. But at the same time, you've got to be mindful of investing in maintenance and periodical upgrades to ensure the property holds its appeal for tenants year on year and maintains its capital value so that when you come to exit the investment, you've got a nice chunk of equity.

Long and short, you need to have a head for figures. You have to be able to account for your income and expenditure and budget properly for the short, medium and long term. You've got to know how to calculate returns and other business key performance indicators (KPIs) so you can track your property and compare its performance to other types of investment.

Having an investor mindset means thinking with your head and not your heart, planning several steps ahead and being quite prepared to make whatever changes are necessary if the property stops making financial sense.

Understanding and Accepting Risk

If you're serious about investing in HMOs as a wealth creation vehicle, you need to get comfortable with taking calculated risks. That means understanding the downsides and potential worst-case scenarios of making an investment and taking steps to mitigate those risks so that you can benefit from the rewards.

So, what are the risks? Here are probably the three biggest ones and how you can mitigate them:

- The property market naturally moves in cycles and is vulnerable to economic shocks, meaning capital values can drop. If you're highly leveraged, you risk falling into negative equity, so if you have to sell, you could lose money on your investment and potentially owe the bank more than the property is worth.

  The solution: give yourself a decent equity cushion by buying something you can immediately add value to through renovation and refurbishment, and make sure you won't have to sell in a downturn by creating and maintaining rental accommodation that will always be in high demand.

- HMOs are highly regulated and falling foul of the law can result in huge fines that could be financially disastrous for you and your property business.

  This is an easy one to mitigate: make sure your property is compliant! (See Chapters 5 and 7.) It will take you some time to understand the national and local regulations that apply to your particular property and tenancy, which can be very different from one local authority area to another, but as long as you set your HMO up right from the start and carry out proper inspections, maintenance and repairs, you shouldn't have anything to worry about.

- With multiple unrelated tenants living in one house, the potential for disputes and property damage is much higher than with a single let. Noise, untidiness, a lack of responsibility and personality clashes are probably the biggest problems, and even one rogue tenant can cause others to leave, meaning you could suddenly have room vacancies. The more disputes there are, the more often your phone will ring and the more time you'll have to spend sorting them out.

  So, start by thoroughly vetting prospective tenants – that's checking their rental background, credit status, employment and right to rent. Have clear house rules and make sure tenants know their responsibilities. Having a great property manager (if it's not you yourself) and making periodical visits can allow you to nip problems in the bud before they become major issues, which also creates a safer and more comfortable environment for your tenants.

As well as risk, you also need to be comfortable with debt. Some people break out in a cold sweat at the thought of owing money, and if you haven't invested in property before, you might think the goal is to always own it outright.

Well, that's probably a good idea if it's your own home, where mortgage payments are simply a liability that cuts into your take-home pay. But when it comes to property investment, the best returns come from leveraging the bank's money by way of a mortgage (more about that in the next chapter), and if you're serious about building a profitable property portfolio, you're going to end up with hundreds of thousands, and possibly millions of pounds worth of debt.

But, as long as you've done your research and made sensible purchases, there shouldn't be anything to worry about. With any buy-to-let investment, you should be making sure the rental income services the mortgage debt, covers all the property-related outgoings and gives you a profit on top. And because HMOs are a high-income strategy that almost negates the risk of voids causing income to drop even to a break-even point, there shouldn't be any danger of you not being able to pay the mortgage every month.

Business and investment revolve around borrowing and leverage, so get comfortable with debt because, when it comes to HMO investing, it's your friend.

Being Happy with a Good Deal

I've met lots of potential investors who can't move forward because they're fearful of getting it wrong, of the deal not being good enough. They've found properties that look as though they'd work as HMOs, but they hang back in case there's a better investment just around the corner. The figures seem to stack up, but the returns could be higher...

Well, I've got news for you. There will *always* be a better deal out there with higher returns. You can spend years looking for the perfect deal, and the longer you spend viewing properties, running the numbers, analysing costs and working out how to mitigate risks and maximise income, the more confused you'll get. Not only that, but you start taking the very best parts of every potential investment and putting them together in your head to create a 'super investment' that probably doesn't actually exist.

Successful investors make deals that are good enough. They do solid research, weigh up the pros and cons, and act. Yes, caution is warranted, but too much caution and fear will only lead to missed opportunities. And while you're um-ing and ah-ing over whether the profit you're looking at on paper is enough profit, you're generating precisely zip.

So, one of my top pieces of advice to anyone moving into HMOs is simply to get started. You're going to make a few mistakes – of course you are, this is a new strategy and you're on a learning curve – and your first investment is almost certainly not going to be your most profitable one. But if you've carried out enough research and analysis to make an informed decision, just get on with it. Get some income rolling in, get some experience in the business, then you can fine tune and make adjustments as time goes on.

A Proactive Approach

Investors are also proactive. Too many landlords still only bother with their property when there's a problem, but the really successful ones anticipate potential issues and take steps to mitigate them from the word go.

For instance, staying on top of rent payments and maintaining good lines of communication with your tenants should help avoid arrears and disputes. And making periodical property checks and carrying out regular routine maintenance means you can identify and perform minor repairs before they become costly problems. Plus, when tenants see that you care about keeping their home in good condition, they're more likely to look after it.

Successful investors also understand that you never stop learning in this business and they make a real effort to stay up to date with what's happening in the market. So, go to seminars, mingle with other investors and landlords, join the National Residential Landlords Association (NRLA) and subscribe to good quality industry newsletters. The more you know, the better you will be at making decisions and coming up with creative solutions to stay right at the top of this competitive market.

Being proactive and staying one step ahead will not only help ensure your HMO remains lucrative, but it should keep your stress levels down as well!

Building Resilience and Adaptability

The property market, the expectations of tenants, laws and regulations all change - sometimes in quick succession! – and you've got to be ready to adapt.

You've also got to be resilient because some of these changes will result in you facing setbacks. That might come in the form of regulatory shock, unanticipated voids, rising maintenance bills, higher mortgage rates...but successful investors don't panic, they adjust, recalibrate and solve the problem.

For example, if you find you're suddenly having trouble letting rooms, you might need to reassess your advertising strategy, upgrade or add amenities or perhaps adjust rents to be more competitive. You may have to modernise interiors to match the current trend, provide creative lease terms, or instal smart home tech to appeal to younger tenants. Being able to see industry trends and respond accordingly can be a real key to long-term success.

Even if there aren't any specific changes happening, the mere business of running an HMO requires resilience. Some tenants can be a pain, always contacting you with queries and complaints; when there are problems between tenants, they can take time to resolve; maintenance and repair issucs may drag on or cost more than expected; prospective tenants might not turn up for a viewing; you may need to chase up contractors; you can go round in circles trying to get a straight answer out of the council housing or planning department...and on it goes...

In all these cases, your patience will be tested and you need to have a way of mentally dealing with that, so you don't get overwhelmed. And the key to not ending up in a ball of anxiety and stress, as with so much in life, is preparedness:

1. Know what the potential problems/challenges are
2. Accept that they *will* happen at some point
3. Work out what you need to do to solve or mitigate the impact of them
4. Put those processes in place now, so they're ready to go

For example:

- No matter how well you budget for maintenance and repairs, they will always be something that breaks earlier than it should or a job that runs over budget. So have a 'rainy day' fund set aside that you can dip into when needed, so you're not panicking about paying bills.

- Tenants will annoy you at times, so work out what your triggers are and how to deal with that irritation. Maybe look into breathwork or mediation practices and take time to learn some negotiation and conflict de-escalation techniques.

Knowing the Value of a Great Team

A big key to successfully overcoming problems and challenges and being able to adapt to the various changes that will be thrown at you, is having the right support team. No matter how confident and capable you are, you can't know and do everything, so tap into other people's expertise.

Property investing is a team effort with sales and letting agents, mortgage brokers, contractors, surveyors, property tax experts, property managers and other investors. So be ready to spend some serious time finding these people in your local area that can provide the professional and personal support you'll need.

I can't overemphasise the importance of working with people you really *like* and seeing them not as service providers, but as members of your team – even though many of them will be outside your own business. These are the people you're trusting to help you make a success of what may be your biggest ever financial investment, and you'll be working with some of them for many years, so be generous and treat them well.

Get to know agents, take them out to lunch and talk to them about your investment business. If they know you're serious and reliable, you'll be the first person they call when a great property is coming onto the market, and you'll get to trust them enough to view a property simply on a phone call. Settle contractors' invoices right away, so that they'll always be happy to fit you in when work needs doing. Pay your property cleaners a little extra so they want to do a really good job for you. Thank your professional advisers and core contractors with a gift on completion of projects and at Christmas.

When your whole support team is motivated to do their best work and invested in helping you achieve your goals and targets, it really does boost your success.

And surround yourself with other investors who are experienced and successful. Spending time with people who share that positive, entrepreneurial, solution-oriented mindset, and who have achieved the things you want to achieve, is hugely encouraging and motivating. As well as being invaluable sources of information that can really accelerate your learning, they make you feel as though anything is possible!

Chapter Summary

If I've done my job so far, you should be well aware that being an HMO investor isn't simple, it's not easy money, it's an ever-shifting landscape, and not everyone is suited to the role.

But if you have the right mindset, you're willing to work hard and keep learning, and you can assemble a high-quality support and advisory team around you, the financial and lifestyle benefits will open up. Over time, you should be able to build a property business that:

a. More or less runs itself day-to-day, requiring less of your personal time
b. Generates consistent ongoing income, and
c. Increases in value year on year to provide long-term financial security

The best and most successful HMO landlords over time are those that are:

- ✓ Entrepreneurial and business-minded
- ✓ Comfortable with calculated risks and "good" debt
- ✓ Resilient and solution-oriented
- ✓ Prepared to adapt to changes
- ✓ Proactive and willing to invest in ongoing learning
- ✓ Motivated to constantly improve – both their business and themselves
- ✓ Good at building relationships
- ✓ Professional
- ✓ Comfortable with knowing what they don't know and willing to harness others' expertise
- ✓ Generous

I'd like to finish by expanding on that last one because it's so important to have a generous spirit. That doesn't just mean being generous in financial terms, it's also about being generous with your time and knowledge. Just as you'll learn from those who have already achieved great success in property investment – "stand on the shoulders of giants", as the saying goes – you will also have skills and knowledge that are valuable to others. So, share your experiences and be willing to help where you can, without expecting anything in return. And if you give freely, it'll come back to you in some way, trust me.

Chapter Three

Research & Analysis – The Numbers

Successful HMO investment relies on knowing your market and carrying out careful research so that you can make sensible, well-informed decisions. Forget buying a property, waiting and hoping for the best – that won't get you anywhere!

Not all property is suited to be an HMO, and there isn't demand everywhere.

Profitability with HMOs depends on three key things:

1. Satisfying a specific type of demand, which means you've got to understand your target tenants: what kind of accommodation do they want, in which locations, and how much are they willing to pay?

2. Understanding local and national laws and regulations around HMOs. Legislation can be a minefield and with local authorities in England permitted to make their own rules around planning and licensing (see Chapter Five), it's vital you don't fall into the trap of buying a property you can't let as you want and need to.

3. Being able to 'run the numbers'. You've got to be clear on your up-front and ongoing costs and be able to forecast and budget for them and know how to calculate and track your KPIs (cashflow, ROI and yield).

Numbers don't lie, and the more research and analysis you carry out, the better armed you'll be to run a sound HMO operation that generates stable, long-term income for you.

Finding Profitable Locations

Choosing the location for your HMO is one of your most critical investment decisions. A fantastic property in terms of size, layout and amenities in the wrong area is only going to be a drain on your business. If you find out too late that there simply isn't the demand for your product, it'll take much longer to fill rooms, and you may have to switch your target tenant type and lower prices. Longer voids and less rental income will have a massive impact on your bottom line and could even make the whole investment non-viable.

Enough of the doom. HMOs, done well, in the right location are a fantastic rental investment. Four of the biggest tenant groups for HMOs are:

- Young professionals
- Workers in the service/healthcare industries
- Factory & warehouse staff
- Students

So you're looking for a town or city with a dense working-age population and a thriving economy - somewhere major employers are investing and growing their businesses. If there's a university or college, that opens you up to student rentals.

The area needs to have excellent transport links and the property itself should ideally be on a bus route with easy access to train stations. You also want it to be near to supermarkets and leisure facilities, and the closer you can be to a hospital, business park, student campus, etc., the more likely you'll have constant demand from the tenants who work or study there.

Analysing Demand

If there's already a successful HMO market in the area, that's a good sign that demand is there. That said, oversaturation is a risk. When too many landlords compete for the same tenants, rental prices can be driven down and the risk of voids goes up. So your challenge is to strike a balance and find a location with both strong demand and room for well-operated, new HMOs to thrive.

The first step is to find some data on demand. You can get a quick overview by going on Spareroom.co.uk and looking at the number of 'rooms wanted' adverts for the location you're considering, versus rooms to rent. If there are at least 50%

more tenants looking than there are rooms available, it's a good sign of healthy demand.

Some further research on Spareroom, Rightmove and Zoopla will allow you to compare the quality of available stock and room prices. Look for multi-lets of between four and six rooms in size and make yourself a spreadsheet of postcodes, property sizes and rents for both standard and en-suite rooms.

Just a note on how long listings have been active... In the sales market, if a property has been sitting online for months, that's generally a sign that it's overpriced or there's something wrong with it. But when it comes to HMO adverts, the age of the listing isn't necessarily a reliable indicator of whether rooms have been let, because some portfolio landlords will keep at least one of their properties permanently active online so they're never short of new enquiries and can fill rooms quickly when they come up.

Finally, speak to local letting agents that deal with room rentals - which not all of them do, so you'll need to do some research first. They're dealing with properties and tenants every day, so can provide invaluable insights into exactly what kind of accommodation and amenities different tenants are looking for, how much they're willing to pay and the locations where demand is greatest. They can also advise you on average tenant turnover and any local trends that might affect your cash flow. The more information you gather, the better prepared you'll be to meet market needs.

Local Planning & Licensing Regulations

A significant factor in the viability of your HMO investment is your local authority – specifically, their policies on licensing and planning.

I'll go into these in more detail in Chapter 5, but the headline is that, while there are national laws, each local authority in

England has the power to set its own licensing and planning rules, meaning they can be very different from one area to another.

Planning regulations dictate the permissions that need to be sought before you convert any property into a multi-occupancy home - and whether you can even operate a property as an HMO at all. This is so councils can manage the mix of housing stock and density of local populations, and make sure areas don't become over-saturated with HMOs.

Meanwhile, licensing conditions state how many occupants you can have before a licence is required and lay out the minimum standards you need to meet in terms of property management and amenities. This will impact both your initial set-up and ongoing costs.

So it's absolutely vital that you check out the local council's policies before you move forward. And it's worth knowing that while some councils have great websites and information is easily available, others aren't so easy to access. I'd recommend joining a local landlord association and chatting to other investors at the earliest opportunity, as that can often be the most efficient way to find out how the land lies.

Financial Forecasting and KPI Calculations

A well-thought-out HMO in a location where there's high demand is only a great investment if the numbers stack up. So you've got to understand the Key Performance Indicators (KPIs) and be able to carry out proper financial forecasting *before* making a purchase, to ensure your investment is both profitable and sustainable.

I spent quite a lot of time putting together a series of spreadsheets with embedded formulae that mean I can just change the variable figures and the headline numbers – income, expenditure, profit, ROI, yields – auto-calculate. If you're not used to using programs like Excel, then get comfortable, because it'll be one of your most useful tools.

Here's what you need to know, figures-wise:

Capital investment

Start by calculating the total amount of money you'll need to invest to get your HMO up and running. That will include:

Acquisition costs:

- Deposit
- Stamp Duty Land Tax (and remember there's a 5% additional rate surcharge on the whole purchase price!)
- Legal fees
- Mortgage arrangement fees
- Survey fees

Ready-to-rent costs:

- Renovation & refurbishment costs, including any planning fees (see Chapter 6)

- Cost of meeting health & safety and fire safety regulations
- Furnishing costs

Take the time to ensure quotes and estimates are as accurate as possible because underestimating these initial costs could put you in a difficult financial position before your property even starts generating income.

Expenditure

Once you understand your upfront capital investment, break down your ongoing monthly expenses:

- Mortgage payments (you'll need a specialist HMO mortgage)
- Insurance (again, you'll need a specialist HMO landlord policy)
- Utility bills (usually included in the monthly rent)
- Council tax
- Maintenance/repairs
- Property management fees (if you're not self-managing)
- HMO licence fee

When it comes to maintenance and repairs, you need to consider both ongoing expenses and an allocation for periodical larger works. So have a separate spreadsheet that lists all the areas that will require maintaining and periodically updating or replacing, and plan ahead for 1, 3, 5, 10 and 'once in the lifetime of the investment' expected costs.

For example, your annual/ongoing costs would include cleaning, gardening, gas safety checks, PAT testing and boiler servicing. Your 3 to 5-yearly costs would include redecorating, replacing smaller furnishings and kitchen appliances and perhaps updating some fittings, like handles, hinges and taps. Beyond that, consider replacing larger items of furniture and appliances, updating kitchen and bathroom fittings and making repairs to the external fabric of the property.

Of course, costs do fluctuate and will increase over time, so once your HMO is up and running, it's a good idea to review your expenditure every 3-6 months and update your figures.

Profit

Once you know how much monthly rent you can charge for each room type you're planning to have – single / double / en-suite – add it up and deduct the total expenditure (actual monthly costs and budgeted allowances). That will give you your monthly pre-tax profit.

I recommend also calculating your net profit by including an allocation for the tax that will be due on your rental income (less allowable deductions). This will give you a much more accurate picture of how much money you're *actually* making, month on month and year on year.

Gross Yield

This is the annual income expressed as a percentage of the property value.

(Annual Rental Income ÷ Property Value) × 100 = Gross Yield

For example, if an HMO generates £3,000 per month (£36,000 per year) and the value is £300,000, the gross yield is 12%.

It's a useful headline figure that gives you a rough guide as to how good an investment one property is likely to be, compared to another, and it's the figure you tend to see quoted in industry market reports and the media.

However, it's only based on income and doesn't take into account either the running costs or how much capital you've had to invest. So, when you're trying to work out if an investment stacks up and whether one potential property purchase will be more profitable and give you a better return than another, the gross yield isn't much help.

Net Yield

This is a slightly more useful figure, as it's based on profit, rather than income.

(Annual Profit ÷ Property Value) × 100 = Net Yield

A strong HMO should generate a net yield of at least 10% after all costs. If it's lower than that, it might not justify the extra effort required compared to a standard buy-to-let.

But while it's an interesting comparison tool and indication of the profitability of a property, the net yield isn't really that important. What's really relevant to you as an investor is your cashflow, profit and overall return on investment. And that brings us to the property's potential to increase in value.

Capital Appreciation
Rental income is one part of your profit; the other is capital appreciation, and this is something that you also need to consider before taking the plunge. That's because one property might generate excellent monthly cashflow, but because of its location or size, it might be unlikely to grow well in value.

Another property might sit at a very average level of monthly profit, but be in a much more desirable location, where there's high demand from both investors and homebuyers. In that case, it might increase in price at a good rate, and the equity growth over time could more than compensate for the lower rental profits.

You can check the sales history of a property on sites like Rightmove and Zoopla, and the Land Registry has fantastic data on prices over time for different property types in each local authority. But if you can find an experienced local estate agent who's been operating in the area for more than 10 years, they're likely to be your best source of information about which properties on which roads are likely to perform best over the long-term.

Once you have an idea of the potential annual growth in value, you can then add this into your income and use that figure to take a look at the overall likely profit and yield.

Return On Investment (ROI)
I've saved the best 'til last! This is the really significant calculation – the one that lets you see how hard your money is working for you. It's the annual profit expressed as a

percentage of the amount of money you've had to invest into the property.

(Annual Profit ÷ Total Capital Invested) x 100 = ROI

So, if you invested a total of £115,000 (25% deposit plus £40,000, purchase, renovation & refurb costs) in a property worth £300,000, which is generating an annual rental profit of £20,000, that's a return of 17.4%. Factor in price growth of, say, 3% per annum and that's another £9,000 you can add to the annual profit, bringing the ROI up to 25%.

You can then use the ROI percentage to compare the overall performance of one HMO with another and also compare your property investment with other asset classes, such as stocks or gold. I'll talk more about scaling up your business in Chapter 9, but it's worth expanding on this now.

25% and even 17.4% ROI is pretty good, but it can be improved significantly over time through remortgaging – jump forward to Chapter 11 for more on that.

Testing the Numbers

Once you've got a realistic picture of your monthly cashflow, profit and ROI, you can play with different scenarios, like how much it would cost to add an en-suite, how much extra rent could you charge for the room and therefore how long it would take to recoup the cost of the work – is it worthwhile? How about if you converted or extended to add another lettable room – what would that cost, and would the returns be worth it?

The other important step is to 'stress-test' your figures against the risks. What would happen if the mortgage interest rate rose by 4 or 5 per cent? What would happen if you had one or two rooms empty for a month? What's your break-even point? You've got to make sure the cashflow gives you enough of a cushion against the possible falls in income and rises in expenditure.

Of course, the exact costs and amount you need to invest will be different for every property you're considering buying and you'll need to do fresh analysis on each potential purchase. This is where a well-set-up spreadsheet comes into its own!

By running all these numbers before you buy, you'll be able to move forward with confidence, knowing you've done everything you can to ensure long-term profitability.

Chapter Summary

HMOs can be incredibly profitable, but only if you do your homework. Most novice investors underestimate refurbishment costs, overestimate rental returns, or forget to plan for contingencies if things turn out badly. Successful investors do their sums, make careful budgets, and plan for worst-case scenarios. So:

- Find an area with solid HMO investment fundamentals: strong local economy, thriving working-age population, commercial business investment and expansion, good transport links, university/college campus, convenient amenities.
- Research online and speak to letting agents to understand rental prices, tenant demand and potential occupancy rates
- Analyse competition to determine if the market is oversaturated or if you can offer a better product
- Check local council planning and licensing regulations to ensure you can operate your planned HMO and understand the costs associated with meeting requirements
- Carefully analyse every potential investment, ensuring you know:

    - The amount of capital you'll need to invest
    - All expenses associated with the property
    - How much you need to budget for maintenance and improvements over time
    - Your tax liabilities and how much you'll need to set aside from your profits
    - Your break-even point – stress-test the income and expenditure figures
    - Yield and ROI, so you can compare it to other properties and investments and ensure your money is working as hard as possible for you

By collecting and analysing all this data, you'll be in a stronger position to make a confident investment decision. The more knowledge you have before buying, the better your chances of running a successful and profitable HMO, so do the research right at the start and set yourself up for long-term success.

Chapter Four

Conversion to an HMO vs Buying an Existing HMO

Now that we've had a strong HMO market in the UK for a couple of decades, there are lots of landlords coming to the end of their investment journey. So, today you have more of a choice around whether to buy an existing HMO or convert a standard single-family home.

Both have their pros and cons - the right choice for you will largely depend on your personal aims, budget and attitude to risk.

Pros and Cons of Buying an Existing HMO

In my experience, most landlords are quite happy to sell their HMO as a going concern with everything included. It's a hassle-free transaction for them and they can keep receiving rental income right up to completion.

For the buyer, taking over an established HMO can be an excellent shortcut to market. It's already configured for multi-occupancy, should be legally compliant and is likely to have paying tenants in situ. As soon as you take ownership, the rent starts dropping into your bank account and you haven't had to put any extra money into the property to get your new investment up and running.

You avoid the inevitable time lag while you gain planning permission and complete refurbishment works, and you don't have to carry out the numerous viewings it takes to fill a brand-new HMO.

Sounds pretty good, doesn't it?

Okay, so let's take a closer look at those key benefits and then what you need to consider, including the possible downsides.

Much lower up-front costs
In addition to your standard costs of acquisition (survey, stamp duty, legals, etc.), if you're buying something that's not currently an HMO, you've got to budget for:

- Gaining necessary planning and building permissions – which may include a planning consultant and/or architect
- The renovation/refurbishment works themselves
- Getting the property compliant with health & safety and fire safety legislation
- Furnishing

Going for a property that's already up and running means you don't have to put any cash in right away, which could easily save you £20k plus. I usually find I want to carry out some minor refurb in the first couple of years, but it's nice to be able to take your time. And from a purely financial perspective, it means you can store up rental profits for a few months to pay for the works – you don't have to dip into your existing reserves.

While we're on the up-front costs, you might be wondering about the purchase price. Surely if you're buying a going concern, not just the bricks and mortar, the seller will be expecting over the market value...

Not necessarily. Although I've come across many landlords that have started off (a bit cheekily!) by asking for more, the reality is that transferring ownership with tenants in place is just as much of a benefit to them as it is to you. And if they were selling to a non-landlord, that buyer would almost certainly be looking to renovate and refurbish, in which case they'd expect to get a 'good deal'. So you shouldn't be paying over the odds for an existing multi-let.

No void period

Both parties win on the income front here. When tenants remain in situ (and not needing to move is a win for them too!), the selling landlord gets rent up to the day of completion, after which it's yours.

Even if you buy a vacant property that requires minimal refurb *and* you arrange to be given access before completion so you can get it ready to rent and conduct viewings, there will almost always be some void period. (Even with the best preparation, this kind of scenario rarely goes 100% to plan!) In my experience, when you're buying a non-HMO, you should budget for it being 1-2 months before you're fully tenanted.

So, taking on existing tenants can definitely be a positive move – you've just got to make sure you're not inheriting any liabilities. Here are 7 steps to ensuring a smooth changeover:

1. Double-check the figures – don't just take the seller's word about profit levels!
2. Ask the seller to confirm that there haven't been any problems with the current tenants and none of them are in arrears with their rent.
3. Meet at least some of the tenants so you can gauge for yourself what they're like and find out about their experience of living in the property. Is there anything they think needs changing/improving or are they happy with things as they are? (This is also your opportunity to introduce yourself and reassure them about having a new landlord.)
4. It's 'tidier' if you can agree to complete on the 1st of a month and ensure tenants have your bank details in plenty of time to make that rent payment to you as the new landlord.
5. Ask the seller to provide you with all tenant-related paperwork, including Right to Rent and credit checks.

6. Although the tenants' existing rental contracts will remain valid, it's a matter of best practice to ask them to sign new ones. This is also something your mortgage and insurance providers may require.
7. Ensure deposits are transferred to you on or as soon as possible after completion.

Is it legally compliant?

If the current landlord has done everything they're supposed to and maintained the property in good condition, it should be legally compliant. However, you still need to make sure you know the laws, rules and regulations that apply to HMOs, both nationally and locally, so you can check that for yourself – there's no shortcut.

That's things like:

- Do the rooms meet the minimum size requirements?
- If the property is licensable, check the conditions of that license have been met
- Are fire safety measures up to date?
- Is the property free from hazards?

Remember that ignorance is no defence, and if it turns out that the property you've bought is non-compliant, you could face fines or even be prevented from letting it altogether!

If the property is in a local council area that has tight licensing rules, and especially if they're keen to control the number of multi-lets, buying an existing HMO might actually be the safest or only option. I'll go into these regulations and permissions in some detail in the next chapter.

Does it meet current demand and expectations?
One of the biggest considerations when you're buying an HMO that's been up and running for a number of years is whether it's still what today's tenants want. You've got to know that when you next need to fill a room, you won't struggle to find a tenant who's willing to pay a good market rent.

A property might be legally compliant and in decent condition, but...

...Does the layout still work? If it was converted 15-20 years ago, the shared facilities might not have been designed in the best way. Are there enough en-suite and laundry facilities? Are the kitchen and bathrooms modern enough? When was the electrical installation last updated and is it suitable for all the gadgets, devices and pieces of equipment your tenants will want to plug in?

When buying an existing HMO, you're constrained by what's already there, and you don't want to have to make major renovations in the foreseeable future to stay competitive. In certain situations, particularly if it's an older property, it can actually cost more to bring an HMO up to standard than it would to convert something from scratch, so you really need to do your due diligence before you buy.

Of course, buying a property that's not currently an HMO is going to be a more expensive and time-consuming venture, especially if you're making changes to the layout, but that extra capital input at the start could turn out to be a great investment.

You can plan the space to fit current demand

Conversion of an ordinary property to an HMO gives you total control of the design, layout and tenant experience. You can research exactly what kind of living space is most desirable and make sure you create accommodation that will deliver the highest rental returns. More on this in Chapter Six: Designing for Cashflow.

And because you're renovating and putting in new fixtures and furnishings, your maintenance costs should be pretty low for the next ten years or so.

Making improvements could boost the capital value

When you buy an existing HMO, the capital value is going to be more-or-less the price you pay for it, and that will then only increase in line with the market.

But if you can buy something that could already do with upgrading and improving and then make a really good job of the work, that's likely to mean an increase in the value. If the gain is big enough and you can refinance, you might then be able to release some or all of that additional equity to cover the cost of the works – hopefully with profit on top!

The best uplift I've achieved within my current portfolio is £41,000, along with an instant monthly profit of £1,416. That was a modern three-floor townhouse that I converted to an HMO with five en-suite bedrooms, housing professional tenants. As of 2025, the capital value is £465,000 and the net monthly rental is £2,650.

Spend Category	Amount
Purchase price	£ 324,000
Purchase costs: professional fees, stamp duty and refurbishment	£144,000
Total capital required	£144,000
Immediate value after refurbishment	£365,000
Immediate profit (Equity created after refurbishment)	£41,000
Rental income	£35,000
All anticipated monthly costs including: mortgage, service charges, Ground Rent, full management, maintenance & allowance for voids	£16,080
Annual Net Profit vs monthly	£16,992 /£1,416 pm

Make sure you understand the local authority planning laws and building regulations you'll need to comply with – and bear in mind these can sometimes take a while to gain. And if you've ever carried out building works, you'll also know that there can be hidden costs, so take the time to really plan the outgoings and have a realistic contingency in your budget.

Professional service providers and specialist contractors

To make sure the conversion is a success, you've got to have the right professionals helping you. Depending on the extent of the works required, that's likely to include:

- ✓ An architect and/or planning consultant
- ✓ A surveyor
- ✓ A builder, ideally one who's already familiar with HMO conversions and the various regulations for space, light and other building regs
- ✓ A project manager, if that's not something you're comfortable doing yourself – it could be the lead builder
- ✓ A plumber
- ✓ An electrician
- ✓ A fire systems expert

I'll talk more about this over the next couple of chapters, but it's really important to understand that you get what you pay for! In my experience, it's well worth spending a little more to get a conversion done right and on time. I can promise you that cutting corners at the outset will come back to bite you in the wallet!

Assessing Properties for Conversion

Not all houses are suitable for conversion and if you buy the wrong one, it can very quickly turn into a stressful financial nightmare. When it comes to the bricks and mortar, here are things to look for in a good prospective HMO:

- ☐ Big enough to fit the number of lettable rooms to generate the required returns (as per Chapter Three), plus suitable shared amenities
- ☐ High ceilings and good natural light
- ☐ Extra rooms that could become lettable bedrooms
- ☐ Large living rooms or smaller reception rooms that could be knocked through to create an open-plan living space
- ☐ A large kitchen
- ☐ An integral or attached garage that could be converted to another room
- ☐ Potential for extension
- ☐ Multiple bathrooms
- ☐ Areas that could be converted into en-suites
- ☐ Space for a laundry room

You can assess all those things for yourself on an initial viewing and a survey should highlight any issues with the fabric of the property in due course.

But before making an offer on a property, go back with an experienced builder and ideally a plumber as well, who can advise you on the feasibility and cost of things like knocking down walls, dividing areas and converting rooms to bathrooms. If you're planning major works, it may be worth paying for a structural survey even before the purchase is agreed, to confirm you'll be able to do what you need to.

Once you've got a good idea of the extent and cost of the works, ask either the selling agent or a surveyor to give you an idea of the end value of the property once it's done. Then run the numbers thoroughly (Chapter Three) to make sure the returns are worth the investment before moving ahead.

Understanding Conversion Costs

The cost of conversion and refurbishment can vary wildly depending on the condition and layout of the property. You might only need to make minimal changes, such as installing fire doors, adding a bathroom and redecorating. At the other end of the scale, the property might need new plumbing, a loft or garage conversion, soundproofing and all the fittings replaced.

Get detailed quotes from contractors – and try to get them to agree a whole-project cost at the outset, so every little discovery or time delay doesn't cost you more. On average, a well-designed conversion will cost between £20,000 and £50,000, but it's advisable to have a contingency buffer of 10-20% in your budget, just in case.

The other expense - which you avoid if you buy an existing HMO – is the cost of legal compliance and licensing. While the

95

licence fee itself might only average out at a few hundred pounds a year, the licence conditions might mean you need to spend more on the renovation, e.g. if you need to provide additional amenities. Meanwhile satisfying fire safety alone can cost anywhere from £5,000 to £8,000.

Then there's the indirect cost of not having rental income while works are being carried out following completion of the purchase. If you buy an HMO that's up and running, you're straight into positive cash flow, but if you're converting, you need to factor an initial void period into your budget. For however long there aren't any tenants in the property, you've got to cover the monthly mortgage payment, utility and service costs, possibly even council tax, all of which eats into your annual returns. So it's massively important to have a tight refurbishment schedule and budget and make sure things stay on track, because every week without rental income is lost profit.

Chapter Summary

Choosing between buying an existing HMO and converting a standard property into one depends on your budget, risk tolerance, and investment goals.

The three big benefits of buying an existing HMO are:

1. Lower up-front costs – you don't have to spend the time and money on conversion, compliance, fitting, furnishing and filling with tenants
2. Income from day one
3. A less stressful rental acquisition (assuming it's running well)

However, you run the risk of inheriting hidden problems and possibly an outdated layout that could be costly to remedy in the future.

If you convert a property yourself, that gives you:

1. Control over the design – layout and amenities – so you can ensure it meets the highest tenant expectations
2. The opportunity to refresh everything and 'future proof' so that you minimise maintenance and repair costs over the next 10+ years
3. A likely uplift in the property value and an 'instant' equity boost – which you could use to lower your mortgage LTV, release to cover conversion costs or invest into another property

Although this option does require a much greater financial outlay and can be time consuming to plan and execute, the long-term benefits should be worth it.

Chapter Five

Planning and Licensing

Over the last decade or so, the government has imposed much more stringent safety regulations and licensing requirements on HMOs. Significantly, each local authority in England has been given the power to set its own planning and licensing rules, which means you've got to know and abide by both the national mandatory regulations and those imposed by your own local council.

And it can be a minefield, not least because while some councils are very good at publicising rules and changes, some are downright dreadful. That means, depending on where you're investing, you might have to go hunting to find out what you can/can't and must/mustn't do, and that can be time-consuming and massively frustrating. But it's something you've got to get right because the planning and licensing rules in your area can make the difference between being able to maximise the income potential of your HMO...and not being able to let out the property at all!

Why do we have these regulations?

Once the buy-to-let market started to boom in the late '90s and early '00s, among the many decent landlords, there emerged a pool of not-so-decent ones. Often referred to as 'rogues', these were (and still are) simply criminals.

Criminal landlords have various modes of operating, but most rely on taking advantage of vulnerable tenants – those that are poor, on benefits, perhaps immigrants...anyone who might find it hard to tick the necessary boxes for a legitimate rental or simply can't afford one. By filling sub-standard, badly maintained, illegally let properties to as many tenants as possible, criminal landlords keep their outgoings low while collecting more income than they should.

The bigger these overcrowded properties are – particularly in terms of the number of storeys – the more dangerous they become for the tenants. And so, as the government has worked hard over the last 15-20 years to raise standards in the private rented sector, they've made deliberate moves to ensure that HMOs remain more regulated and subject to higher health and safety standards than single household lets.

Even when HMOs are well-run, there's the fundamental fact that a property which might ordinarily have had three or four occupants acting as one household, now could have six or seven plus, all doing their own thing. And when those extra heads of population start to multiply, it's not necessarily good for every area, which is why individual councils have the right to decide whether and how strictly to limit both the number of HMOs and the number of occupants in each property.

On the whole, the rules are good for you!
While some landlords view tight regulation as a hardship, it's actually been good news for the HMO market. As long as the rules are enforced, below-par properties and inexperienced landlords that aren't up to operating at the required level are squeezed out, leaving a market that's made up predominantly of legally compliant, well-presented and well-managed HMOs.

With the general bar set higher these days, the reputation of HMOs has improved almost beyond recognition. Once seen as the cheap, no-frills alternative to a whole-property rental, many tenants are now choosing all-inclusive room lets and communal living because they like the convenience, the amenities and the social aspect, and average rents are much more in line with the rest of the market.

Does my HMO need Planning Permission?

Planning regulations put buildings into different classes. Single household residential homes are categorised as 'C3', while HMOs are 'C4'. The question here is whether you are required to apply for planning permission for change of use.

If your local authority is simply going by the national rules, you may be able to operate a property as an HMO with up to six tenants under 'permitted development' rights, meaning you can switch class without going through the planning process. If you want to house seven or more tenants, you're

likely to have to seek formal planning permission (which is one reason for not having more than six tenants).
However, it's not quite that simple in practice.

Each local authority has the power to impose an 'Article 4 Direction', which allows them to restrict or remove permitted development rights. You tend to find Article 4 applied in high-density areas, university towns, and locations with housing shortages – areas where there's a need to prevent an oversaturation of HMOs and ensure properties meet local planning standards.

That might mean you need to make a planning application for change of use for any size of HMO. The council might place a limit on the maximum number of tenants you can have in the property, and they may even stipulate how many parking spaces you must provide in order to comply. But here's the kicker: with the Article 4 tool, a council could simply reject your planning application entirely, meaning you can't operate the property as an HMO at all.

If you fail to check and simply move ahead with getting your HMO up and running, the council could require you to apply retrospectively. If permission is refused, you will be required to return the property to a single household dwelling.

So one of the first things you need to do when you choose an area for investment is check the local council's planning policy and find out whether any Article 4 restrictions apply. If you don't, you risk making a big financial mistake and possibly facing a costly and time-consuming legal battle.

What is the Planning Application Process?

You will need to submit detailed plans that include property specifications and potential impact assessments. The application must demonstrate that the property will provide adequate living conditions, meet fire safety standards, and not negatively affect the surrounding area. The more your application aligns with local housing needs and regulations, the better the chance of approval, so it's well worth speaking to other local landlords and researching the council's current policies.

The whole process can take several weeks or even months, depending on the council's workload and any objections from neighbours. If residents believe that an HMO will lead to increased noise, parking issues, or a decline in community standards, they may submit formal objections. Councils take these concerns seriously and may deny applications based on community feedback. If your application is rejected, you may need to revise your plans, provide additional supporting documents or appeal the decision. All of this is likely to delay your project and increase overall costs.

For that reason, I'd advise you to work with a planning consultant who specialises in HMO developments. These professionals understand local regulations, common council concerns and best practices for HMO conversions and can help you prepare a strong application that addresses potential objections before they arise. Although hiring a consultant adds to the up-front cost, it can save time and reduce the risk of rejection, making it a worthwhile investment.

Do I need an HMO Licence?

Mandatory licensing was introduced in 2006 for properties of three or more storeys, housing five or more tenants that formed two or more households. Then, in October 2018, the three-storey element was dropped.

Now, as it stands under national law, if you have a large HMO – housing five or more tenants from more than one household

– you need a licence for the property. In most cases, if there isn't any other licensing scheme in place within your council area, applying for and securing a licence should be a pretty straightforward process.

But, as with planning, local authorities have the power to dictate their own policy and can impose 'additional licensing' on HMOs. This means they can require any size of HMO to be licensed – and the conditions of any HMO licence can vary.

Additional licensing can be applied to the whole of a council area, a particular ward, or sometimes even just part of one street. Licensing schemes tend to run for five years (although it can be less) and they can be brought in at any time. That means you can have several schemes in force across a single local authority, all starting and ending at different times!

(On top of this, councils can impose 'selective licensing' schemes, which can require any privately let property to be licensed, HMO or not.)

If your property is subject to licensing and you're found to be operating without a valid licence, you can be fined an unlimited amount, and the council could ban you from letting until you get one. You could also be handed a rent repayment order that requires you to pay back up to 12 months' rent to your tenants. So, as an HMO landlord, you've really got to make sure you stay up to date with what's going on in your area.

You'll need to apply to your local council, which should have information about the process on their website. The cost of both the application and the licence will vary from one area to another, but as a rough guide, the fee will be somewhere between £700 and £1,500 for a five-year licence. Renewal (which must be done before the licence expires) is generally cheaper than a new application and some councils give discounts if you're in a landlord accreditation scheme.

When you average out the cost over five years, it's really not that expensive, and it does benefit you if tenants are reassured that you're doing things by the book and their home has been 'approved' by the council.

Licence conditions

For any licence, you'll need to show that the property is suitable for the number of occupants in terms of size and facilities, and that the person/agent managing it is a 'fit and proper' person.

You'll also need to send a copy of the gas safety certificate to the council each year, make sure smoke alarms are installed and properly maintained, and provide electrical safety certificates as requested.

In addition to these specific licensing conditions, your property must meet minimum property standards and comply with specific health & safety and fire safety regulations, which I'll cover in Chapter Seven.

Once they've reviewed your application, the council might come back with some extra conditions, such as asking you to make some upgrades or provide additional facilities, but this is unlikely if you've done your homework before the refurb.

All in all, if you're running a decent HMO, this should just be a bit of extra admin.

What Else do I Need to Know About Local Authority Powers?

Your local authority essentially oversees and regulates all privately rented properties in their area. They could inspect your HMO at any time and if tenants aren't happy with standards in the property, they can report you to the council. And, as with any property or resident, if neighbours have an issue with noise or any kind of anti-social behaviour, the council can take action.

As long as you maintain the property well, comply with legal minimum standards and any licence conditions, and manage your tenants properly, you shouldn't have any problems.

However, it's important to know that for breaching any letting regulations, the council can issue a civil penalty of up to

£40,000. (Increased from £30,000 under the Renters' Rights Act.)

If a breach is considered serious enough – for instance, if you've put your tenant in danger – the council can take you to court, where you could be given an unlimited fine and even banned from letting property altogether.

Those are worst-case scenarios. What's more common are things like improvement notices, which councils can serve if the property fails an inspection or tenants have complained about living conditions. This requires you to bring the property up to standard within a specific timeframe and if you don't comply, they're then likely to issue a fine.

Chapter Summary

Planning and licensing are critical aspects of HMO investing that ensure your property operates legally and safely, and that neighbourhoods aren't impacted negatively by this type of accommodation.

Securing necessary permissions may seem like a hassle, but it's a vital step in protecting your tenants and the long-term viability of your investment.

- ☐ Research the local authority planning policies and regulations before you invest:
  - Is there an Article 4 Direction in operation?
  - Does your HMO require a planning application for change of use, or does it fall under permitted development?
  - What are the likely criteria for a successful application?

- ☐ Work with experts that can help you secure planning permission and establish your HMO in a legally sound way

- ☐ Does the council have any additional licensing schemes in operation?
  - Apply for a licence
  - Ensure you meet all the licence conditions

- ☐ Manage and maintain the property to ensure it continues to operate at a high standard, meeting all national and local health, safety and fire requirements

Although it will require some financial investment and professional guidance – not to mention patience at times! - taking the time to navigate all this correctly right from the outset will save you from potential legal disputes, fines, or even forced property closures. Ultimately, compliance will help ensure that your HMO operates smoothly and successfully for years to come.

Chapter Six

Designing for Cashflow

Designing your own home revolves around your personal preferences, style and taste. But when it comes to the design of your HMO, it's primarily about strategy.

This is a financial investment, where property is simply the vehicle for delivering returns, so every refurbishment idea, room setup and design choice should support that ultimate goal of profitability.

Creating a visually appealing home is a big part of attracting tenants, but you've got to balance your spend with the returns your finished product will be able to generate. And, while you need to design a layout that maximises the revenue potential, that doesn't mean squeezing as many lettable rooms as possible into the space – it's got to be a comfortable and practical home for your tenants.

The perfect balance exists somewhere between affordability, financial viability, function, and tenant comfort. Proper design and good quality renovations at the outset will minimise the amount of time and money you'll need to spend on maintenance, and help keep turnover and voids low – which should result in decent, stable cashflow.

I've already written extensively about this part of HMO investing, alongside my friend and fellow investor, Nick Fox, in our book, 'HMO Property Renovation & Refurbishment Success'. It's available on Amazon – just scan the QR code below to access the listing.

Optimising Layouts for Income

Every square metre in your HMO matters. Your research will have shown you how many lettable rooms and facilities you need to provide for the investment to stack up, so when you view a property, you should know exactly what you need the space to accommodate.

Start by studying the existing design to see where there might be 'wasted' space that could be put to better use. For example:

- Is there a large living room that could be split, or a separate dining room that could be repurposed as a bedroom? Tenants tend to spend most of their time in their private bedrooms, so the communal living area doesn't need to be huge.

- Is the kitchen big enough to create a comfortable seating/dining area that could accommodate all the tenants? If so, you may not need a separate living room at all and might be able to gain two (or more) bedrooms by redesigning the existing reception rooms.

- Is there a large built-in cupboard or space in a bedroom that could be converted into an en-suite if that would enable you to charge a premium for the room?

- Could part of a hallway or landing, or some other recess become a shower room?

- Could a loft or attached/integral garage be converted into a bedroom?

If you can redesign the existing structure to provide one or two extra lettable rooms, you may be able to turn an average potential return into an exceptional one.

In many cases, you can create additional space that can be utilised legally and comfortably as another bedroom by moving walls or re-articulating doorway positions. However, while you're being creative, you've always got to bear in mind your tenants' comfort and safety – and your legal obligations. Not all rooms can be converted, and ventilation, fire regulations, and daylight must not be compromised.

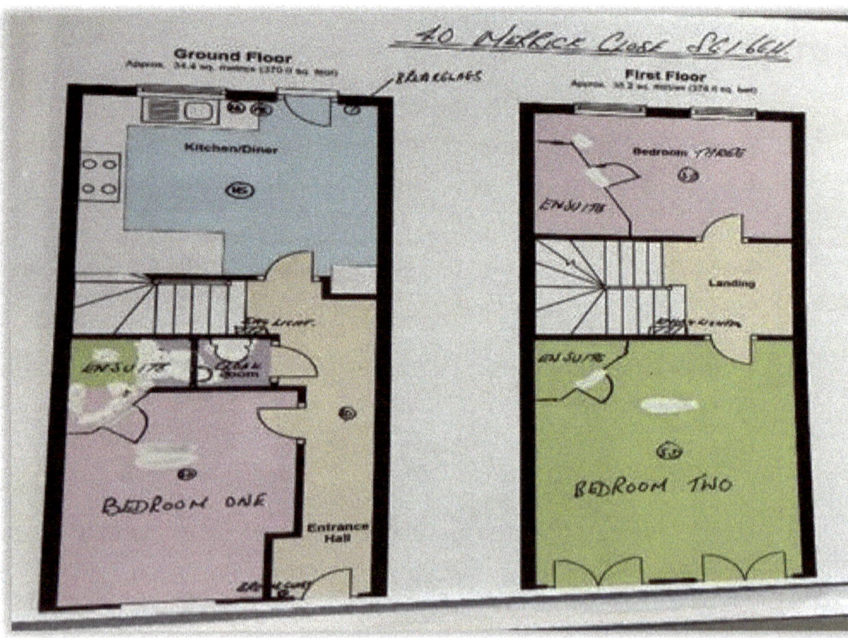

One important thing to know is the legal minimum room sizes. Just because you can get a bed into a space, it doesn't mean you can use it as a bedroom! As it currently stands, a room can't be let unless the floor area is at least:

Single bedroom - 6.51 sqm
Double-occupancy room - 10.22 sqm
Child's room (under 10 years) – 4.64 sqm

And the ceiling height must be at least 1.5 m. Any floor space with a ceiling height of less than that cannot be included in the minimum size calculation.

So, if you're considering converting a loft or a room within the eaves of a property, be sure to measure the space very carefully. If you go ahead with a purchase on the basis that you've got six lettable rooms and one is later found to be non-compliant (and therefore you can no longer let it), that could have a massive impact on your profits.

While you're looking at where you could add extra rooms and facilities, such as a laundry room (always ideal to have somewhere tenants can dry clothes without attracting mould elsewhere in the property!), remember that it's not all about the number of rooms.

In many cases, larger rooms attract better quality tenants, who are willing and able to pay a premium for more space. A well-designed, light and airy room will always be more desirable than one that only just satisfies legal minimum standards.

Many tenants will also happily pay more for an en-suite, especially in HMOs with high occupancy, where shower times in shared bathrooms can become an everyday nuisance. So, if space and plumbing configurations permit, aim to add a couple of en-suite bedrooms to each of your properties. Even if there isn't the space for a whole en-suite, a private washbasin or mini-WC can still boost rental appeal - anything offering more privacy and comfort will earn you extra pounds.

Once you've got an idea of what rooms and facilities you can have and where, think about the flow of the property. Will tenants have adequate privacy? Will they be in easy reach of shared bathrooms or kitchens without intruding on other tenants' space? Can communal areas be easily accessed at all times? A well-designed property will attract and retain better tenants, enable you to charge a good level of rent, and help ensure strong, consistent cashflow.

Cost-Effective Renovations

If you're not up for a major project or you don't have a huge amount of capital available to invest, don't panic - renovating an HMO doesn't have to cost a fortune.

The trick is in knowing exactly where to spend your money and where you can cut back without compromising the appeal of the accommodation or the profitability of your investment.

Let's start with what you ***can't*** scrimp on. The fabric of the building, heating, plumbing and electrics all have to be 100% sound. If they're sub-standard in any way, this will cause you problems down the line that will hit your profits not only in terms of the cost of remedial works, but also in lost rent if you have to temporarily move tenants out. So it's well worth investing in professional contractors and decent quality materials for the core structure of your property.

Then you can move on to more surface-level improvements with the décor and fixtures. Making considered changes in key areas can revamp and refurbish a property without leaving you broke.

Bathrooms and kitchens are a big selling feature for any tenant, and in an HMO these rooms are going to get a lot of use, so it's worth investing in decent, modern upgrades. That said, you don't need to spend an arm and leg.

In the kitchen, carefully chosen mid-range products can give you the look and longevity you need. If existing kitchen unit carcasses are solid, you might only need new cupboard and drawer fronts, and you can find reasonably priced composite worktops that are long-lasting and chic. In terms of appliances, again, mid-range white goods should last a good five years and it's really not worth paying a lot for them, as HMO tenants don't tend to be brilliant at looking after them!

In the bathroom, if the basic suite is in decent condition, you may be able to achieve a updated look simply by replacing taps, shower heads, shower screens and tiling. Install LED lighting that will be energy efficient and can create a bit of a 'wow' factor. Importantly, fit decent extractor fans that come on automatically to help reduce the likelihood of condensation and surface mould – hugely common in shared houses.

Flooring-wise, durable laminate is best for communal areas - it should last well and is easy to keep clean. Most tenants still prefer carpet in their bedrooms but go for something in a mid to dark neutral colour that's designed for high-traffic areas and won't show small marks. In bathrooms and kitchens, sealed laminate or vinyl tiles are a cost-effective option, but if you can afford a ceramic or porcelain tile, that's a long-lasting solution that will give you a better look.

Redecorating the walls is a relatively simple and affordable way of updating the look and feel of your HMO. A new coat of paint immediately brightens rooms and makes them appear cleaner and more welcoming. Neutral colours like pale white, pale grey, cream and soft beige help make rooms feel light and airy and have broad appeal to tenants. At the same time, a feature wall painted in a bright or rich colour in the kitchen and/or living room can really give your rental some personality and pazazz!

In kitchens and bathrooms, use specialist water-resistant, anti-mould paint, and it's sensible to go for a wipe-clean product in high-traffic communal areas such as hallways and landings.

When it comes to fittings, careful upgrades pay dividends. You don't need to spend a lot, but on the other hand, budget products are easily damaged and can look pretty awful after just a few months of use, so fit decent quality door and cupboard handles and curtain rods. Replace older plug sockets with USB ports, make sure all bedrooms has plenty of power-points for charging multiple devices, and install energy-saving LED bulbs throughout the property to save energy and create a warm and welcoming feel.

Furnishing & Balancing Profitability with Tenant Comfort

A well-designed HMO should be focused on two outcomes: maximising rental income and making tenants feel safe, comfortable and happy. Happy tenants that can see you care about giving them a nice home will generally stay longer, pay their rent on time and keep the property in good condition.

The key to profitable yet comfortable design is to know your ideal tenant. Different tenants have different priorities, and accommodating their specific preferences and needs can enable you to charge better rental returns.

For example, many young professionals are looking for a spacious, peaceful room, ideally with an en-suite for privacy, and a nice communal area. Meanwhile, students tend to be happy as long as there's decent Wi-Fi, a study desk in their room and good public transport links nearby – they might not be so fussed about the communal spaces.

So, when you're deciding where to spend money, think about renovating for your tenants' benefit. Ask yourself: will this upgrade make life easier and better for them? If not, you might be better off spending that money elsewhere.

So, what do you need to provide in terms of furniture and décor to give your tenants the kind of home they'll want to stay in?

Bedrooms

You need to provide all the basic furniture you'd expect in a hotel room, without the bedding itself: a bed with a headboard and mattress, bedside tables, a wardrobe, some drawers and (ideally) a desk.

You should also provide lamps and light fittings, a mirror and curtains or blinds. I always also put up some kind of picture or artwork, just to make the room feel more homely.

Kitchen

The exact amenities you'll need to provide may depend on the council's particular licensing conditions, but the food storage, preparation and cooking facilities need to be appropriate for the number of tenants. As a minimum, you'll need:

- Oven and 4-ring hob
- Fridge & freezer (I allow one fridge shelf and half a freezer drawer per tenant)
- Dishwasher
- Microwave
- Toaster
- A kettle (I usually provide two)
- Plates, bowls, glasses and cutlery
- Basic cooking and baking equipment and utensils – pans, trays, blender, etc.

Communal living room/area

There should be enough furniture to comfortably accommodate all the tenants at once and somewhere they can sit to eat. So you could go for a couple of large sofas or a sofa and some chairs, plus a dining table. If there isn't a huge amount of space, some comfy seating plus a breakfast bar might suffice, or you could simply have a table and chairs. It really comes down to your tenant types and how much time they're likely to spend in the house outside their rooms.

You should also provide some side tables, suitable lighting and a smart TV – and remember you'll need to get a licence for it (though tenants are responsible for gaining licences for watching TV in their own rooms).

Laundry

It's ideal if you can create a laundry room in the property, with a large capacity washing machine and tumble dryer. You'll also need to provide an iron and ironing board, a vacuum cleaner and a sweeping brush.

Storage

Lots of tenants want somewhere they can store bulky personal possessions, such as sports equipment and suitcases, outside of their bedrooms. So it's a good selling point if you can offer them access to a secure garage, loft space or lockable outside shed.

Extras

Overall, you're working to create an environment that's functional and pleasant for your tenants. There's no need to go overboard, but having mirrors, pictures and even low-maintenance plants and some ornaments in the communal areas can help create a homely feel.

And although you'll be arranging a regular cleaning service for the communal areas, I think it's good practice to encourage the tenants to keep the place up to scratch by providing a stock of products such as dishwasher cleaner, anti-scale gel/spray, carpet & upholstery cleaner, bathroom cleaner and toilet gel, plus some cloths.

A clean, comfortable home is a happy home, and happy tenants are less likely to move and take better care of the accommodation you've provided. Happy tenants are also likely to spread the word and some of my best new tenants have come to me through recommendations from current and former house sharers.

Chapter Summary

Proper planning of the layout and design of your HMO is an integral part of setting you up for long-term investment success. Conversely, if you rush this step, cut corners where you should be investing, and fail to understand your market, you could end up wasting money and with a property that's a financial drain rather than an asset.

Understanding your likely return on investment (see Financial Forecasting in Chapter Three) and careful budgeting are key to balancing your spend on refurbishment. Do your research, take advice from letting agents and other landlords, and always use specialist contractors to ensure the quality of the work.

Ultimately, the profitability of your HMO depends on attracting and retaining good tenants who are willing to pay a premium rent for a high standard of shared accommodation. And that's not only about location and facilities, it's also about whether the property makes them feel safe, comfortable and happy.

So, step back and look at the property from a personal angle – are you genuinely happy with what you're creating?

My benchmark is, quite simply: would I have my sons or daughter live here? If the answer is yes, then I know I've done my job.

Chapter Seven

Amenities Standards and Fire Safety Regulations

Since the Housing Act came into force in 2006, a huge amount of legislation has been introduced to raise health and safety standards in rented properties. Some years it's felt like we've only just got one new regulation straight and then we've been clobbered by another change to get our heads (and wallets) around.

There's no doubt that the cost of compliance has had an impact on profits, not to mention the time it's sometimes taken to understand and effect legal changes. And now the Renters' Rights Act is about to give us another shake as the measures come into force, beginning with the new assured periodic tenancy from May 2026.

That said, making sure homes are of a better standard and safer for tenants is obviously a good thing, and as the quality of HMOs has risen across the board, it has helped boost rents. There's no question that investing in HMOs is still, on average, the most profitable investment strategy in terms of cashflow.

And even ahead of the upcoming new legislation, I think we're pretty much there when it comes to providing tenants with decent, safe homes, so complying with the changes that'll be coming in over the next few years should be pretty straightforward.

This chapter is all about the minimum standards for HMO accommodation, amenities, health and safety, and fire safety. As I mentioned in Chapter Five, while standards are now high across the whole buy-to-let industry, the rules are even tighter for HMOs, simply because the risks are greater when you have multiple unrelated people living together in bigger properties.

Like planning and licensing, standards and regulations can be a bit dry, but bear with me, I'll do my best!

Right, deep breath, let's dive in.

Essential Amenities for Tenants

A well-equipped HMO should provide all the essential amenities to ensure that tenants have a comfortable and convenient experience. The better the amenities, the higher the chances of attracting long-term tenants and keeping voids to a minimum, and the better your rental returns should be. But in providing those amenities, it's a fine balance between tenant needs, your budget (the spend has to make financial sense), and your legal responsibilities.

Kitchen

One of the most important amenities is a fully equipped kitchen – ideally, a kitchen/diner. Since multiple tenants will be sharing this space, often at the same time, it has to include sufficient cooking appliances, equipment, storage, and seating arrangements to accommodate everyone.

In terms of the basics, there should be at least one oven, hob, refrigerator and sink for every five tenants, plus crockery, cutlery and glassware. There needs to be sufficient counter space for food preparation, and enough cupboard space for each occupant to store their food and kitchen supplies. On top of that, these days tenants expect a decent kitchen to include a dishwasher, freezer, and one or two microwaves, kettles and toasters. Then, depending on the tenant types, you might want to include extras for added appeal – such as a coffee machine and blender for young professionals.

Bathroom

The minimum requirement is typically one bathroom for every four tenants, but providing extra bathrooms can make the property more attractive and much more functional. If you have a house full of working adults, they're likely to be getting ready for work at a similar time, so the more en-suites and shower rooms you can include, the easier their mornings will be.

Bathrooms should have proper ventilation to minimise the chance of mould build-up, reliable hot water access, and high-quality plumbing to prevent maintenance issues. When you're refurbishing, I highly recommend fully tiling the walls and

floors to make cleaning easier, and ensure the pipework is easily accessible, such as via a removable panel.

Laundry facilities

Laundry facilities are a must-have in HMOs and, in my opinion, you should plan to include a dedicated laundry room. One of the most unappealing things about HMOs is seeing washing hanging in communal areas, and by giving the tenants a specific space where they can dry their clothes, you not only improve their living experience, you also massively cut the chances of surface mould appearing in their bedrooms.

If you have five or more tenants, you really should provide two washing machines to prevent long waits. Some landlords choose to install coin-operated models to cover electricity and maintenance costs, but my opinion is that washing machine usage should be part of the all-inclusive rent. However, I do recommend putting in a coin-operated tumble dryer! Have a ceiling-mounted drying rack – one on a pulley, ideal for bedding – and provide two or three free-standing airers.

Communal living room/area

While tenants have their private rooms, and that's where many choose to spend most of their time, a comfortable shared area can foster a sense of community and improve the overall tenant experience. There should be enough seating for all the tenants and somewhere to eat, and - even though they're likely to have digital entertainment devices in their rooms - you should also provide a smart TV.

As you're likely to have upholstery and soft furnishings in this area, it's important to note that everything you provide must meet fire safety standards. That means relevant items must have an attached label that confirms the item is 'match' or 'cigarette' safe.

High-speed WiFi

Once seen as a 'nice extra', a fast and reliable internet connection is an absolute must. Many tenants rely on high-speed Wi-Fi for work, study and entertainment, and HMOs with weak or slow internet connections do tend to struggle to attract and retain tenants.

There are likely to be times when every occupant is using the internet, possibly all streaming, so make sure your provider knows this and can guarantee a reliable service. Be prepared to pay a premium and install boosters if necessary to ensure that all rooms receive a stable signal.

Door locks

Tenants need to be sure that their personal bedroom is secure, but they also obviously need access to front and back doors and any other on-site secure storage. Rather than having to give them multiple keys, we use a Garrison master suited lock system, where keys can be customised to open certain doors within the property.

So, each tenant has just one key that opens their door and the main doors to the property. If they lose the key, we can change the barrel and reset another key.

The system is also really handy for property management purposes, as it means our maintenance and cleaning teams only need a single key to access every area and property – there's no need to carry a massive bundle and have the annoyance of constantly trying to find the right one for each door.

The most important thing is that tenants have a 'keyless escape' – i.e. they don't need a key, code or device swipe to get out of the property in case of a fire. So, whatever means of access you choose to install, it must be a 'thumb-turn' lock from the inside.

Outside space and storage

Even if it's just a patio with a table and chairs, you need to provide your tenants with an outside space where they can relax in the fresh air. The importance of this was highlighted during the pandemic and it's something that's stayed with us. If you have a garden, that's great for tenants, but bear in mind that you'll need to employ a gardener to maintain it – it's not the tenants' responsibility.

With many tenants getting around on bikes, you should provide somewhere they can securely park/store them. Tenants often also have bulky items like sports equipment that really isn't suitable to be stored in their bedrooms, so aim to provide a lockable shed or garage – this is a big bonus for tenants.

General Safety Standards

Whatever type of tenant you have, they'll expect a comfortable, well-equipped living environment that meets modern standards. At the same time, councils enforce strict rules on room sizes, shared facilities, and overall property conditions to ensure tenants' safety and comfort.

So as long as you understand your target market and comply with the law, you should end up with happy tenants and high retention rates – and avoid being handed any penalties by the council!

As an overarching rule, under the Homes Act 2018, you have to make sure your rented property is fit for habitation (i.e. safe and comfortable for your tenants) at the start of a tenancy and that it remains in good condition throughout the let. There are national regulations that all HMO landlords must follow, then each local council may have its own standards and guidelines for licensable properties.

Here's an overview:

Overcrowding
Overcrowding can lead to poor living conditions and health issues, so councils have the ability to limit the number of occupants in any property and minimum room sizes have been set to ensure each tenant has sufficient personal space.

A single bedroom must have a floor area of at least 6.51 square meters and a double-occupancy room at least 10.22 square meters. To be included in the calculation, the ceiling height of the area must be at least 1.5m. In addition, living rooms, kitchens, and bathrooms must be large enough to accommodate the number of tenants in the property (more on these amenities in the next section).

If a property fails to meet these size requirements, an HMO licence application is likely to be rejected, which would mean reducing the number of tenants and/or making costly adjustments.

Ideally, try to get someone from the housing department of the local council to visit the property in the early stages of the renovation/refurb, so you can show them exactly what you're proposing. Then if you need to make any changes, hopefully it won't be too tricky or disruptive to the works.

Preventing damp and mould

Surface mould/mildew and damp patches caused by condensation has always been one of the biggest problems in rented properties – if you're already a landlord, you'll know all about it!

Black mould isn't just unsightly, it's dangerous. Even touching spores can cause skin irritation and allergic reactions, and if they're inhaled, it can lead to all sorts of health problems, including asthma attacks and severe respiratory infections. If damp and mould are allowed to spread, they can damage furniture and belongings and can even cause mite infestations.

The law says you have to keep your property free from hazards (that's the 29 hazards specified in the Housing Health and Safety Rating System). So, when you're refurbishing, make a point of ensuring there's decent ventilation in the property, such as trickle vents in double-glazed windows and extractor fans in the bathroom and kitchen. The layout of the property as a whole should allow air to circulate, and each room must have windows that can be opened and sufficient natural light.

If you spot damp and mould, it's your responsibility as the landlord to get rid of it and do your best to fix the source issue – even if you're 100% convinced it's your tenant's fault!

I always recommend having a notice board somewhere in the communal space, where you can pin up various house rules and information for your tenants, which should include a reminder about the importance of heating and ventilating, and wiping up condensation if it starts to pool on windowsills.

Services

You've got to make sure that all the equipment (pipework, fittings, etc.) for supplying the property with water, sanitation, gas and electricity is kept in good working order, as well as all the sanitary fittings, e.g. sinks, baths, showers, toilets. There must also be adequate heating and hot water.

Gas and electrical safety

As with any rented property, you need to have an annual gas safety check carried out to make sure that boilers, gas stoves, and heating systems are safe to use. This must be done by an engineer who's on the Gas Safe register and if you need to make any repairs to gain the certificate, you need to have those carried out as soon as possible. A copy of the current certificate must be provided to your tenants and the local council.

Although it's not a legal requirement, it's worth having an annual boiler service as well to help keep it running properly – remember, the safety check is a separate thing.

The full electrical installation has to be inspected at least once every five years to ensure wiring, sockets and appliances are in good working condition. A copy of the written record must be given to the tenants. Although PAT testing isn't yet mandatory, you are obliged to make sure all the electrical equipment you provide is safe, so it's best to have those tested annually.

Waste management

HMOs tend to generate a significant amount of household waste, and if you don't provide tenants with adequate bins, bags and waste storage facilities, you can quickly end up with hygiene issues and complaints from neighbours.

The council may require you to provide larger bins, recycling facilities, and designated waste collection areas, and you may have to pay for an additional rubbish collection service if the council schedule isn't frequent enough. Long and short, you need to do everything you can to prevent overflowing bins and avoid encouraging pest infestations.

Security
Security and tenant well-being are also part of HMO safety standards. External doors and windows must have proper locks and security measures to protect tenants from break-ins or unauthorised access – and this is something your insurer is likely to insist on. All my properties also have motion-activated lights at the front and back or side doors.

Internally, all communal areas must be well-lit - again, it's a good idea to have motion sensor lights in the hallway and on landings – and you must make sure there aren't any hazards such as loose floorboards or broken handrails.

Fire Safety: Systems, Materials, and Checks

This is one of the most critical compliance areas for HMOs. Due to the higher number of unrelated occupants, the risk of fire-related incidents increases in shared housing, so regulations are tighter than for single-let properties.

Each local authority is responsible for setting and enforcing its own fire safety rules, so the exact requirements can vary slightly from one area to another. However, there are basic minimum standards that every HMO should satisfy.

The first step is to carry out a written risk assessment – this is a legal requirement – and it must be updated annually. You can do this yourself if you feel confident enough, or you can pay a fire safety professional, which will cost around £400. I'd say it's a good idea to have it done professionally the first time, then you can use this as a template and update it yourself going forward.

Every HMO must have a mains-powered, interconnected fire alarm system with battery back-up. You need to install smoke alarms in every bedroom, hallway, and communal space, and a heat detector in kitchens, where the risk of fire is greatest. These alarms must be hardwired with a backup battery to ensure they function even during a power outage.

You're legally obliged to make regular checks to make sure the system is working properly, and it should be maintained and serviced according to the manufacturer's instructions. The local council can ask to see records of the checking and servicing at any time, so make sure you keep records.

Fire doors are another crucial safety measure. All bedroom doors and kitchen entrances must have fire doors that are fire-resistant for at least 30 minutes, and the doors should have automatic closers to prevent fire from spreading. I fit fire doors for every room and in rooms like the kitchen and living room where it's not particularly pleasant or convenient to have the doors permanently closed, I fit holders to the wall that automatically release when an alarm sounds.
Note: You must impress on tenants the importance of **not** propping open fire doors!

There should also be multi-purpose fire extinguishers on each floor, which should be serviced annually, and a fire blanket in the kitchen.

A side note here... Every fire officer I've spoken to has said that only people who have received proper training or instruction should attempt to use fire extinguishers. For the most part, you should just get out of the property and leave any firefighting to the professionals! So, while it's your duty to provide extinguishers, remind your tenants that their lives are the most important thing – you've got insurance for the property.

Escape routes must be clearly marked and free from obstructions, and windows and exits must be easy to open in case of an emergency. You might also need to put emergency lighting in hallways and staircases to guide tenants to safety if a fire occurs at night.

Finally, somewhere in the communal space you need to put up clear instructions about what tenants should do in the event of a fire – where to exit, where to assemble and who to call.

Ultimately, if something goes wrong and you end up in court, you've got to be able to prove you took all reasonable steps to ensure your tenants' safety. So the best way to make sure you're meeting your fire safety obligations is to ask a local council HMO enforcement officer or fire safety office to visit the property before you move any tenants in and take their advice.

Maintenance and Repairs

You have a legal obligation to keep the property in good condition, free from hazards, and all the services and equipment in good working order. This is where having a proper inspection and maintenance schedule, and reliable contractors, pays dividends.

If leaks, breakages and blockages aren't dealt with at an early stage, they can quickly become big problems that are much more costly to fix.

I check all my properties 3-4 times a year, inside and out, and make sure my tenants know to call as soon as they spot any issues. It's a legal requirement to provide all tenants with contact details for the person managing the HMO, and to have them on display in the property – another piece of info to go on your communal noticeboard.

We also operate a 24/7 call centre to manage any maintenance or emergency issues for our tenants & properties – everything from lockouts to power cuts and blocked pipes to floods.

Staying on top of things not only protects the value of your investment and keeps you on the right side of the law, it also reassures your tenants that you care about making sure they have a decent home – and what do we say about happy tenants...?!

Although the vast majority of landlords are pretty good at organising repairs, it's worth knowing that if a tenant reports a problem and you don't get it sorted out, they could report you to the council. If you still don't fix things and the matter spirals, you might end up with a rent repayment order and a fine. Not a path you want to go down.

Chapter Summary

Although meeting safety standards requires time, effort and financial investment, it is essential for the long-term success and sustainability of any HMO business, and it's something you need to take seriously.

By following all these safety and health regulations you're ensuring that tenants enjoy a safe and comfortable living space and protecting your investment. Staying on top of your compliance obligations will help avoid tenant disputes, prevent unexpected legal costs and should mean the property remains in good condition, holding its appeal for tenants and protecting the capital value.

There's an awful lot of information to absorb in this chapter, so I won't try to summarise it here, but it is worth highlighting the regulations are a moveable feast. The government seems to have the rental sector under permanent review, and there will be several changes we'll need to make to the way we let and manage our HMOs over the next few years as the various measures in the Renters' Rights Act come into force.

Added to that, local authorities can introduce new rules and chance requirements at any time and sometimes without much, if any notice, so you've got to make sure you have a reliable way of staying up to date with the latest regulations. I recommend joining a local landlord association, and being a member of the NRLA also gives you access to a great support network and resources.

Chapter Eight

Marketing Your HMO

Tenants are the lifeblood of your investment. You're not making any money until they've moved in and are paying rent, so you need to make a real effort to keep the gap between completion on your purchase and full occupation as short as possible.

Even before the property is finished and ready to rent, you should be thinking about marketing your HMO and working on getting the right people in through the door.

You've got to be clear on your target market and know exactly what they're looking for, then craft a listing that stands out and grabs their attention. There's a lot of competition out there and you want a room in *your* property to be top of everyone's wish list.

Once you've succeeded in generating an enquiry, the in-person selling starts. How do you make sure the viewing turns into a room sale? Do you even want to let to that person – are they right for the property? What questions should you be asking and answering?

If you've never sold before, you might find this part uncomfortable, in which case, it may be better to use an agent for the let - more on that in Chapter Ten. But if you're up for the challenge, here goes.

Crafting the Perfect Property Listing

Building an ideal listing begins by stepping into the shoes of your potential tenant. What would make *you* stop while scrolling through page after page of room adverts?

The best listings are to-the-point and – this is the crucial bit - inviting. Every other HMO landlord out there has got a room in a house that has shared facilities, and loads of them will also be charging an all-inclusive rent that's either the same level as yours or lower.

Your job is to stand out by crafting a listing that really sells the benefits of living in your house. Of course, you've got to list the basics of what's on offer, but every landlord is doing that. So, you need to highlight the things that really speak to the emotional side of the process of choosing somewhere to live and sell the experience, not just the bones of what's there.

At the same time, don't overload your listing. You just need to grab tenants' attention and make them book a viewing – you can discuss the details in person – this is all about dropping the right breadcrumbs.

Here are the key elements of your listing:

Photos

The top two things that matter are the headline and the photo, but since the human brain processes images way faster than words (somewhere between 6 and 600 times faster), let's start with your photos.

Aim to photograph all the rooms once the property has been fully refurbished and before any tenants move their things in. Ideally, take pictures twice - once during the daytime on a bright, sunny day, and then late afternoon/early evening with lamps and other lighting on to give it a cozy feel.

Pro tip: Often, you'll get the best exterior shots of the building if you take them around dusk with the lights on inside.

The quality of the image and what's in it says a whole lot to your tenant about how much you care about what you're selling. So, stage the bedroom that's for rent by making up the bed and perhaps putting some greenery in there to give it some life and take a few different angles.

Make sure the communal living area and kitchen are both clean and tidy, with some attractive accessories. A floor-standing plant in the living room and bowl of fruit or vase of flowers in the kitchen might be a bit clichéd, but they work! Put on lights in the bathrooms and don't forget to snap the garden with some outdoor furniture nicely arranged.

Most room listings will only show one photo on the search results page, so choose whichever looks most appealing, bedroom or living room, and include as many of the communal parts and other bedroom angles as you can (SpareRoom allows 10).

Heading

Your title is the first thing people read, so make it specific and descriptive. For example, instead of the dull "Double room for rent", maybe you could put "Spacious en-suite double rm in shared house" – something that, along with the photo, will make people click on the listing. The rent and whether it's "all bills incl." will also be displayed on the results page.

Main selling points

Once they've clicked, give a summary of the key features – the best things about the property that not every landlord will be offering, such as:

- Super-fast broadband
- Laundry room
- Rear garden with dining patio
- Bi-weekly cleaning of kitchen and communal space
- Secure bike storage / off-road parking

Description

This is your opportunity to give tenants a real sense of what the property is like. Tenants are looking for privacy, security, modern amenities, convenience, space and comfort – so sell those things and try to tick off as many of their 'wants' as possible, not just the things they 'need'.

Start with a summary of the whole property – here's one of mine:

A three-storey terraced town house, converted into a six-bedroom HMO professional house share, that has recently been extensively refurbished, creating a modern, bright and spacious home, with off-road parking.

Then on to the specifics of what they're paying for. Be as descriptive as you can, so don't just say, "furnished double room"; say it's a large, private room (list dimensions) with a comfortable double bed, wardrobe, bedside tables and drawers. And make sure you include any details that improve the tenant's experience, like USB plug sockets, blackout curtains and ergonomic desks. Such features suggest a level of thoughtfulness and attention to comfort that tenants will appreciate.

If there isn't an en-suite, tell them how many shared bathrooms, shower rooms and WCs there are in the property, e.g. one full bathroom and two further shower rooms with WCs, all modern and fully tiled.

Go on to describe the rest of the shared accommodation, e.g. bright, modern, well-equipped shared kitchen with plenty of cupboard storage and a large breakfast bar; cozy living room with smart TV; private rear garden with patio, table and chairs, plus a secure shed providing additional storage.

Location is one of the most powerful selling points, so highlight local amenities like shops, gyms and parks, and if the property is on a bus route or close to a train station. Many houseshare tenants rely on public transport links, so it's also worth giving the estimated time it takes to walk or commute to popular destinations like universities, offices and attractions.

Be as truthful as you can in your description and include any firm house rules or prohibitions, e.g. no smoking or no parties. It's also important to be clear about the kind of environment you're offering – e.g. 'suitable for young working professionals'. The last thing you want is a wasted viewing.

Rent details Specify the deposit and weekly or monthly rent, and list exactly what "all inclusive" covers – usually gas, electricity, water, council tax, WiFi and cleaning.

A note here: If you're concerned about an all-bills-included rent, don't be. It's the only way to operate when you have tenants who are all moving in and out at different times, and as long as you install things like a thermostat limiter and don't give them free run at a tumble dryer, the rental premium should comfortably cover the actual bills.

And having just one fixed accommodation payment each month makes budgeting much easier and less stressful for tenants, particularly if they're on a low income.

Using Digital Tools and Platforms Effectively

Marketing your HMO today involves more than just putting up a 'For Rent' sign in the window and sticking a small ad in the local paper. The vast majority of tenants start their property search online, so it's crucial that your listing appears where they're looking.

SpareRoom (spareroom.co.uk) is undoubtedly the best platform to market & sell your rooms, as it's dedicated to house and flat shares and is where most people go first. It's pretty cost-effective and easy to use and provides a very consistent stream of decent quality enquiries.

If you're marketing to young professionals, it's also worth considering listing on **OpenRent** (openrent.co.uk), which tends to particularly attract that type of tenant. I've also tried Gumtree in the past, but to be honest, there was such a diverse range of respondents, most of which weren't suitable, that it just wasn't worth the admin.

Although you can use the same basic information, you might want to tweak your adverts according to the preferences of the site's users. For instance, on SpareRoom, tenants are likely to appreciate a description that focuses on the quality of the room, shared living spaces and the type of housemates already living there. Meanwhile, for professional tenants browsing on OpenRent, it's worth emphasising the property's amenities, location, and suitability for work-life balance.

Social media can be just as powerful in reaching potential tenants. Facebook Marketplace and local property groups are fantastic for connecting with people who are looking for housing in your area. These platforms allow you to interact with potential tenants directly, answer questions, and even negotiate terms.

Then Instagram is great for showcasing the aesthetics of your property and creating a visual narrative that draws people in. If your HMO has stylish interiors, modern furnishing features or impressive views, posting on Instagram with appropriate hashtags can help attract younger tenants who appreciate these details.

If you manage multiple properties, social media becomes even more valuable and it's well worth considering creating an account or page specifically for your HMOs. By posting consistently and engaging with your followers, you can build a brand that potential tenants trust. Sharing photos, videos, and testimonials from current tenants will give your properties a personal touch and provide social proof that you're a reliable landlord.

It's also important to understand how to use these tools efficiently. For instance, when boosting a post on Facebook, make sure to target the right demographics. You can select criteria such as age, interests, and location, so your ad reaches individuals who are most likely to be interested in your property. Similarly, when using paid listings on platforms like Zoopla or Rightmove, make sure your property description is optimised with keywords that tenants are searching for.

Automation tools are another game-changer for landlords looking to streamline their tenant-finding process. With the help of automated services like viewing booking apps, tenant screening tools, and messaging platforms, you can manage enquiries more efficiently. Apps like WhatsApp Business allow you to quickly respond to tenant queries, while property management platforms help you organise and track leads. A fast response time is critical in the competitive rental market, and using these tools ensures you don't miss out on potential tenants. Being organised and responsive is a clear sign of professionalism, which builds trust and encourages tenants to commit to your property.

Lastly, always analyse the results of your marketing efforts. Most digital platforms provide analytics tools that allow you to track how many people have viewed your listing and clicked on it, so you can see which platforms are working best for you and where you need to improve.

Turning an Enquiry into a Sale

Advertising is just the first part of marketing – the bit that grabs someone's interest. Once you've got an enquiry, you've got to turn that prospective tenant into someone who's actually keen and able to sign the tenancy agreement!

1. **Respond quickly**

   Generally speaking, if someone's making an enquiry about a room to rent, they're ready to sign up, and possibly even ready to move in. They'll be actively looking at all potential options and won't hang around waiting for you to get back to them.

   So you need to answer enquiries pretty much as soon as you get them. A quick reply shows you're proactive and interested in letting out your home, and suggests you'll be professional and reliable in other areas of the letting process.

2. **Be available and flexible for viewings**

   While you're trying to fill rooms, you need to accept your life is no longer your own! Well, not quite, but you must be prepared to prioritise viewings. Working adults are generally only available in the evenings and at weekends and they often want to see the property as soon as possible, so keep your diary flexible and be as accommodating as you can. Remember, if they can't see your room this evening, they'll probably have a couple more they can view instead.

3. **Be prepared with all the rental agreement info to hand**

It's worth putting together an information sheet for interested tenants that outlines the information you'll need from them if they want to take the room and, ideally, run through it with them on the phone beforehand. That's things like:

- References
- Permission for credit checks
- Documents required to satisfy right to rent checks
- How much the deposit is and how you'll protect it
- The rent amount and when it's due
- The rental agreement
- House rules
- Inventory

4. **Be friendly and professional**

Tenants want to know they've got a decent landlord, and you need to be as sure as you can that you've got a good tenant who's going to fit in with the other people in the house and communicate well with you.

So, when you meet them for the viewing, be warm and friendly and take an interest in them. Don't interrogate them (!) but do make an effort to ask about their work, their family, their hobbies, etc., so you can get a feel for what kind of person they are.

Show them all the amenities and benefits of the property and reassure them about regular cleaning and maintenance. Ask if there's anything else they need and consider reasonable requests. For example, if they'd like a desk in their bedroom and they're planning to stay for the foreseeable future, it's probably worth providing one.

The more you can show tenants you care about their comfort and happiness, the more likely they are to treat the property well and stay longer – and all the starts from your first meeting.

5. **Don't be afraid to say no**

   Property is a people business and I'm a big fan of trusting your gut. If you take on a tenant who ends up causing trouble – anything from falling out with their housemates to not paying their rent and damaging the property – it may be tricky to get rid of them. Other perfectly good tenants might hand in their notice, and you could find yourself in a whole world of financial and legal pain.

   There's nothing that says you have to accept an application from a tenant, and you can simply say you didn't feel they were right for the property.

   Note: Whenever you're dealing with a tenant application, you must be mindful of discrimination laws.

If the viewing goes well and you decide to accept the tenant, great – you've filled a room! Now on to the next one!

Just one last thing before we finish off on marketing. Sometimes, you'll find there's a room in a property that's harder to let than the others. It might be a small double, or have a sloping ceiling, or perhaps not have the best layout... Whatever the reason, you need to get a tenant in there because an empty room is lost profit.

Any room will let at the right price, so my advice is to come down on the rent if necessary. You don't have to drop the price on the advert, but if a prospective tenant's not committing when you're showing the room, just ask what they're not sure about. If it's the price, offer them a discount. You're better off taking £550 instead of £600 a month versus having a void.

Chapter Summary

Good marketing is a vital step on the path to establishing a robust HMO property business. To maximise the income potential, you've got to operate at full occupancy with the right kind of tenants, so you need to establish a reliable way of sourcing those tenants.

That means having a stand-out listing with eye-catching photos and a punchy write-up that highlights the best things about your rental, then making sure it gets in front of the right people. SpareRoom is likely to remain the frontrunner on the portal front, with OpenRent not far behind, but if you're trying to appeal to twenty and thirty-somethings these days, you'll need to gen up on your hashtags and reels, and work on promoting your business on social media as well.

"Content is fire. Social media is gasoline."
Jay Baer, author & inspirational marketing speaker

If you're not too hot on Insta, it might be worth finding someone who is and incentivising them to run social media advertising for you - maybe give them commission for every lead that converts to a tenancy...?

The final stop on the marketing circle (and it is an ongoing loop) is the viewing, where you're selling not only the room and property, but yourself as well. This is where the relationship between you and what could be a long-term tenant begins, so start as you mean to go on. Be honest and open, and show that you're running a professional rental business, and that should give tenants the confidence to sign on the dotted line.

Chapter Nine

Tenant Management

One of the big worries newer landlords have about HMOs is the tenants. Usually, these are valid concerns, like tenants not getting on with each other and landlords having to referee disputes; nobody taking responsibility for shared tasks such as taking out rubbish and keeping communal areas tidy; groups of young folk living together having parties, damaging the property and upsetting the neighbours...

And sure, it can be a nightmare if you don't have the right people in your house. That's the right individual tenants and the right combination of people, which all starts with your vetting process.

Managing tenants in an HMO is more than just collecting rent each month. It's about building good relationships, creating a respectful atmosphere, and making sure everyone in the house feels comfortable and safe. A well-managed property not only keeps tenants happy but also reduces the number of complaints, late payments, and unexpected move-outs.

So, you need to set clear rules and expectations from the very beginning. People come from different backgrounds and may have different ideas about what's normal or acceptable. With a proactive approach builds trust and makes managing easier for everyone involved.

Setting Expectations and Agreements

Effective communication is the foundation of any successful landlord-tenant relationship, and it begins with setting clear expectations right from the start. And I do mean the very start.

That's why it's so important to make sure your advertising is a faithful representation of the accommodation and what the rent includes, as well as any specific house rules, e.g. no smoking anywhere on the premises and no loud music or parties after 10pm. Word of mouth is one of your greatest and most reliable forms of marketing, and the last thing you want is for a tenant to come for a viewing and feel you've wasted their time by not being entirely honest about the property.

And that includes the type of environment you're offering. For instance, if you're renting out an HMO designed for quiet, professional tenants, make this clear in your advert. Or, if your property is suited for students or shift workers who might have irregular hours, it's important to state that. When potential tenants know the type of household they'll be joining, they can make an informed decision and you're more likely to attract tenants who will be the right fit and get on with each other.

The viewing is when they should feel reassured about the quality and set-up of the HMO, and about you as their landlord. This is when you need to cover how you expect everyone to treat the property and highlight what steps you've taken to make their lives easier and keep the property in good nick: plenty of bathroom and kitchen facilities, the bi-weekly cleaner, waste/recycling facilities, laundry facilities and so on.

Tenant vetting

This is an area where landlords differ in their approach. When you're handing over an entire property to a tenant, it's vital to carry out full referencing, but when you're only letting a room, you may feel it's less of a risk.

One check you've got to make is a right to rent check. This is legally required to ensure the prospective tenant has the right to live in the UK. Then your mortgage lender or insurance provider may require you to carry out a particular level of vetting, such as a credit check or work reference.

As standard, I do a right to rent check, get a reference from their previous landlord, take their employer's details and ask for their last three months' bank statements. That lets you see their regular income and outgoings so you can judge whether the rent's affordable. Beyond that, I trust my gut in terms of whether they seem like a decent person and will be a good fit with the other tenants in the house.

Vetting the tenant is not only important for minimising the risk to you, it also lets the tenant know that you're running a professional operation, and you expect them to do things by the book as well.

Once you're happy to offer them a room, arrange the check-in and send them over a copy of the tenancy agreement to look through before they sign.

Check-in

You should have covered most of the key points about the house at the viewing, so the check-in isn't so much about orientation, it's about showing the tenant that you care and giving them the opportunity to ask any questions.

That said, one thing I always particularly emphasise at check in is how much space has been allocated for each tenant in the kitchen – you'd be amazed how many arguments start there! Allow one cupboard, one fridge shelf and at least half a freezer drawer per room. I've never gone as far as sticking numbers on doors and shelves, but it is something you need to monitor, believe it or not.

Another crucial part of setting expectations is explaining how tenants should report any maintenance or repair issues. The simpler and more straightforward the process, the more likely tenants are to report problems early. If they're new to renting, they might not be aware of the risk of damp and mould – as I've already said, this is one of the biggest health hazards in HMOs – so make sure you advise them on using extractor fans and regularly opening windows, particularly in their bedrooms.

It's also essential to set boundaries regarding communication outside of regular hours. For instance, be clear that non-emergency messages should only be sent during business hours – believe me, some tenants have no qualms about firing off texts in the middle of the night! And let them know how quickly they can expect you to respond – I always say within half a day, unless I'm on holiday.

Give them an idea of how often you (or your property manager) will be visiting the property, whether for routine inspections or any necessary repairs. Unlike with single lets, where tenants have the exclusive use of the whole property, with an HMO you can come and go from the communal areas as often as you like. However, you don't want your tenants to feel as though they're being spied on, so I'd recommend making a routine monthly check and putting the date of the next check up on the communal notice board. That way, they'll be reassured you're looking after the property, but you're not trying to spring a visit on them or catch them out.

Go over the house rules, which it's a good idea to include in the tenancy agreement, and then have them sign the agreement there and then – assuming you've sent a copy to them ahead of time.

And while it's not necessary to do a detailed inventory, I always take photos of the room and contents, paying attention to any existing marks or damage, so there's a date-stamped record.

Finally, if there are other tenants around, be sure to introduce them!

House information file

To reinforce your expectations and help your tenants out, put together a printed house manual that includes essential information and guidance, including:

- Emergency contact details
- A list of house rules
- Wi-Fi information
- Bin collection schedules
- User manuals for any equipment you've provided, e.g. for the TV
- Local taxi numbers and bus timetables
- Local take-away menus

I also put up a noticeboard, either in the hall or kitchen, with contact details for the house manager, the bin collection schedule and info on the next routine checks, plus details of any maintenance/repair works – who will be attending and when. Keeping the tenants up to date on everything will foster trust and respect and reassure them you're looking after them.

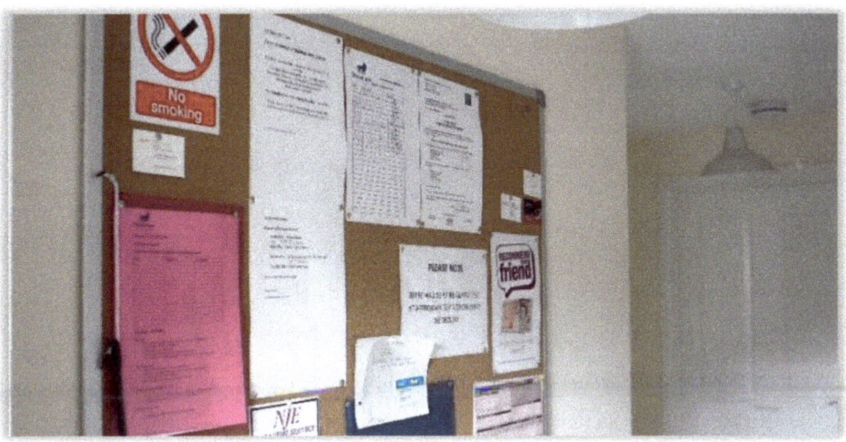

Consistency is key
From the moment the tenant moves in, make sure all your communication, from your responses to maintenance requests to how you handle complaints, is predictable and consistent. If a tenant knows they can rely on you to keep your promises - whether it's answering a question promptly or maintaining the property to a high standard – they're more likely to respect the rules and take care of the property themselves.

Setting these expectations early and consistently following through should ensure that everyone is on the same page and help avoid misunderstandings down the line.

Conflict Resolution Strategies

Even in the most well-managed HMOs, conflicts can arise. After all, you're bringing together individuals that might have different lifestyles, habits and personalities, all sharing the same space. Differences in routine, cleanliness and even personal opinions are common sources of friction, not to mention attitudes to noise and shared responsibilities.

So, you need to be prepared to mediate conflicts fairly.

When it comes to managing difficult tenants, you've got to be professional, consistent in enforcing policies, and know when to call in the law if necessary. Having a calm, structured approach to handling disputes will not only help restore peace but also safeguard your reputation as a responsible landlord. It's important not to panic when conflict emerges. Whether a tenant brings a problem to your attention, or you just sense some tension during a routine visit, the first thing to do is listen. When people are upset or annoyed, they want to feel heard. Encourage tenants to express themselves respectfully and reassure them you're impartial.

If several tenants are involved, it might be a good idea to set up a house meeting. Giving tenants the opportunity to openly discuss their concerns with your third-party perspective and input can make a significant difference and you can usually resolve things there and then. If house rules were violated, it could be a simple case of reminding them why the rules are there and that they did all agreed to them when they moved in.

For more serious or ongoing conflicts, stronger measures may be necessary. Anti-social behaviour - such as making unreasonable noise, bullying, aggression and violence – is a ground for eviction and you are perfectly within your rights to ask the tenant to leave. And make sure your tenants know that if they feel threatened in any way by another tenant, they can call the police.

If you do need to issue a written warning to any tenant or begin eviction procedures, it's essential to maintain professionalism and fairness throughout the process. Keep accurate written records of all conversations, messages, and actions taken during the conflict resolution process so that you can prove, if necessary, that all steps were followed properly.

And if you do have to evict a tenant, it's advisable to take advice from a lettings specialist legal professional before doing anything, because if you don't follow the correct legal process, the eviction could be thrown out in court and you'll have to start again from scratch. To avoid any potential liabilities, you could just outsource the whole thing by using an eviction company, such as Landlord Action.

Although conflict resolution is an important skill, preventing conflict in the first place is always preferable. This is why thorough tenant screening, clear agreements, and regular check-ins are essential in creating a harmonious living environment.

Set the tone early by being clear, consistent, and approachable. Make sure your tenants know they can come to you with any concerns, no matter how small they may seem. By fostering an open and supportive environment, you encourage tenants to communicate with you directly rather than letting problems fester, and hopefully minor issues can be resolved before they develop into bigger conflicts.

Ensuring Long-Term Tenant Satisfaction

When you've gone to the trouble of finding good tenants, you want to hang on to them for as long as possible. I'm going to keep saying it: happy tenants are likely to stay longer, treat the property with respect and recommend you to others. That keeps your voids to a minimum, ensures your income remains steady and saves you time and money.

And long-term tenant satisfaction doesn't require you to offer luxury amenities or extravagant services. It's just about being reliable, fair, and responsive – both in dealing with tenants and maintaining their accommodation at a decent standard.

You don't need to (and nor should you!) become best friends with your tenants; but checking in with them every few months to ask how things are going can help you spot any issues early. It's also a good way of getting a heads-up if they're thinking of moving on, so you can be prepared for re-filling the room.

Make your tenants feel at home

Having a safe property that's well kitted out with modern fittings and all the equipment and appliances your tenants might need is the foundation of providing them with a good home. But you also need to think about creating a welcoming and comfortable environment that feels homely.

What are the thoughtful little touches that don't cost much, but can make all the difference in attracting and retaining tenants? Some ideas for you:

- Side tables beside seating
- Lamps in the lounge area and bedrooms
- Bathroom storage
- Plenty of mirrors to add light and depth

- Low maintenance plants that you can ask your cleaner to water
- Extra plug and USB sockets in bedrooms
- A basic stock of cleaning products
- A Christmas tree – and small gifts for everyone
- A barbeque
- Some card and board games

Maintain the property well

There's no getting away from the fact that maintenance and repair costs are higher in HMOs than in single lets. With multiple tenants in the property, all living as individual 'households', kitchens, bathrooms and communal areas naturally get greater wear and tear than if a single family lived in the house, and you've got to keep the place up to scratch.

So, make sure you plan ahead and budget properly for the cost of things like redecorating, appliance and equipment breakdowns and general repairs. Then find some reliable contractors that you know will respond quickly to your call and do a good job (prompt payment of their invoices usually works!).

If you let the property get tatty and don't fix little problems quickly, your tenants will become dissatisfied. If you don't care, why should they? They'll be less motivated to keep the house clean and tidy and more likely to leave. They may also be tempted to report you to the council, which could result in an inspection and an improvement notice or even a fine.

But if they see you responding promptly when something goes wrong and know that you're prepared to invest in fixing things properly - it won't just be a 'bodge job' – that will reassure them about the quality of both their home and their landlord.

Get feedback

Finally, don't underestimate the value of asking your tenants for feedback. The best way to know what's working and what could be improved is by asking the people who live in the property.

You could send out a short survey once or twice a year or arrange a visit at a time when most of the tenants are likely to be there and talk to them face to face. What do they like and is there anything else they need? Sometimes tenants make suggestions you might not have considered, and incorporating their ideas might improve the living experience for everyone – plus, they'll appreciate you asking their opinions and taking their ideas into account.

Chapter Summary

Successful tenant management begins with your marketing and continues all the way through the tenancy, which could last several years. A lot of people still think of room rentals as very temporary living arrangements, but that's just not true. My longest sitting tenant has been with me for 10 years, and I've got another who's coming up on 9 years in the same room. I do sometimes worry that I've made them too comfortable!!

Tenants who know what's expected of them, and what to expect from you, are more likely to feel happy and secure in their living arrangements. Being consistent - in both your management of the property and your dealings with them – and maintaining open lines of communication, shows them you're reliable and approachable, and that will lead to a smoother tenancy for both of you.

Chapter Ten

Letting Agent vs. Self-Management

With any rental property, you've got a choice to make about whether to manage it yourself or hire a letting and managing agent. Both options have their pros and cons, and your decision will depend on your personality, the time you have available, and your experience and level of knowledge.

When it comes to HMOs, the management demands ramp up. For each property:

- You're usually handling five or six separate tenancies instead of one – that's five or six times the admin of a single let
- Tenants will move in and out at different times, and you can have multiple new tenant finds and lets through the year
- There's more wear and tear on the property, so you'll have more maintenance and repairs to carry out
- Queries will come at you from five or six (or more) separate individuals, rather than one household
- You'll need to manage and mediate any disagreements and conflicts between tenants

- Your legal health and safety, fire safety and management obligations are greater than with a single let, so there's more to know and stay on top of

If things go wrong and you fall foul of the law – whether that's forgetting to renew a licence or unwittingly breaching fire safety regulations – the local council could fine you up to £40,000 or take you to court. And make no mistake that councils pay much more attention to HMOs than single lets. Just Google 'landlord fines' and you'll see that the biggest ones are always for HMOs.

So, if you're going to self-manage an HMO successfully, you need to understand it's a part-time job with a variable shift pattern! I'd say that if you're in full-time employment, or already have demanding self-employed commitments, outsourcing the letting and management of your property is probably the way to go.

But if you have flexible working hours and you're willing and able to spend the time needed to stay on top of your obligations, it can be a really rewarding venture.

Letting agents can take care of everything for you, from finding tenants and collecting rent to handling maintenance and legal compliance. This can save you a lot of time and stress, and give you peace of mind that your property and tenancies are being handled by professional specialists. However, there's a cost to their services, and not all agents are equally skilled or reliable, which is why it's so important to understand what they offer and how to choose the right one.

On the other hand, self-managing your HMO gives you full control. You'll know exactly what's happening in your property, build direct relationships with your tenants, and potentially save money on management fees.

Let's take a closer look at the main considerations.

Pros and Cons...

Cost and Value

For a full management service, agents typically charge between 12% and 15% (plus VAT) of the monthly rental income. Taking an average HMO monthly rent of £3,000, that's £432 - £540 a month out of your profits.

Each of my properties generally delivers at least £1,500 monthly profit, so you're talking about a third of that going to an agent. If you think that sounds a lot, it is, and from a tangible money-in-money-out perspective, it's much more cost-effective to handle things yourself...

...but you've also got to put a value on your own time. You can spend anywhere from 20 to 30 hours a month on administration, dealing with tenant issues, making checks and dealing with property maintenance – often at inconvenient times. What hourly rate would you expect to receive for that?

Legal knowledge and responsibility

As I've hopefully made clear, legal compliance is a complex and important aspect of operating a safe and decent HMO. There's a lot to get your head around, which takes time and effort, and you really can't afford – financially or reputationally – to get caught breaching the rules.

So, if getting to grips with that kind of detail isn't your thing, and you're at all concerned about being able to stay on top of legal changes, use an agent. Although, legally, the buck for most things stops with you as the landlord, by signing a contact with an agent, you are effectively abdicating the responsibility for much of the ongoing compliance to them. And where you need to take action or responsibility for certain obligations, a professional agent will be able to advise and update you.

Streamlining admin

Operating HMOs involves a lot of admin, from vetting tenants to tracking communications and rent, and keeping maintenance and compliance records. If you're self-managing, you need to be very organised, so it really helps if you get some personal satisfaction from it. If things like scheduling, filing, checking, and chasing people up tend to frustrate or annoy you, then get someone else to do the job on your behalf!

Agents are doing the job day in, day out, for multiple landlords, so they have all the systems and processes in place to manage lets as efficiently and cost-effectively as possible. Something you might have to spend three hours on as as individual landlord, might take a specialist HMO agent 15 minutes.

I should say, when you're making the decision about whether to DIY or outsource, if you're planning to build a portfolio, you'll be putting together your own in-house team down the line. So, if you're competent enough to handle management, and you'd just rather not, don't worry, you'll be able to hand the admin over to someone else at some point.

Control over your HMO

While you might be keen to offload the job of letting and managing to someone else, it's worth really thinking about whether you're happy to let go of the ability to decide who's living in your property and exactly how it's managed. When you're outsourcing, no matter how professional the agent, you need to accept things might not be done quite as you'd like.

For example, although they'll carry out all the necessary referencing, an agent might not be quite as discerning as you about the type of tenant they put in a shared house. And sometimes even the best agents won't necessarily inspect a property as often as you would, or ensure the property is cleaned to the same standard as you might expect.

Self-managing puts you firmly in control of how your HMO is run. You get to make tweaks here and there as you go along to maximise rental profits, and being able to build personal relationships with your tenants can lead to higher satisfaction and better retention levels.

Choosing a Reliable Letting Agent

Unlike in Scotland and Wales, letting agents in England don't currently have to be licensed or trained, so they're certainly not all the same. And while good agents are worth their weight in gold, a bad one can damage your reputation and income, so you've got to do your research.

Probably the most important thing is to use an agent that's a member of one of the industry's self-regulating bodies, ideally Propertymark. The organisation requires principal people in the agency to achieve various formal qualifications in lettings, and team members have to undergo regular training, so you can be as sure as possible that the people looking after your HMO know what they're doing.

While every agent in the country has to legally join an Ombudsman scheme, Propertymark also has a best practice code of conduct for members and provides legal support. So you should get a good standard of service and if anything does go wrong, you've got an extra level of redress via Propertymark.

Not every agent handles HMOs because they're more demanding than standard lets, so you might not have a huge choice, especially if you're not in a big city. And if you're going for the professional tenant market, rather than student lets, you'll need to do a bit more homework to find the right agent for you.

The best place to find out about agents is usually your local landlord association. Talk to other landlords and investors who have been letting for some time – they'll have sussed out which agents are worth the money, and which should be avoided! Pay attention to what people say about their communication, honesty, and how quickly they solve problems.

Arrange to meet a couple of agents and go armed with questions. Find out:

- How they screen and select tenants
- What their fees include
- How often they inspect properties
- How they handle maintenance issues, complaints and tenant disputes
- Their process for chasing late rent payments

Read the management agreement carefully before signing anything. All agents should clearly explain all their costs and services up front, but make sure you understand exactly what's included in their fee and what would incur an extra charge, e.g. making additional property visits to comply with licence conditions or amending a tenancy agreement.

Ultimately, listen to your gut and choose an agent you like and feel comfortable with. You're trusting them to look after one of your most valuable asset and ensure it generates decent returns over the long term, so you need to be confident that they know what they're doing and have your best interests at heart.

Tools and Tips for Effective Self-Management

If you decide to manage your HMO yourself, you'll need the right tools and systems in place to keep organised. The good news is that modern technology has made self-management easier than ever and now there are lots of apps and platforms designed specifically to help landlords save time and stay compliant.

Some of the most popular property management platforms are Landlord Vision, Arthur, Property File and COHO. They let you store tenancy agreements, log expenses, send rent reminders and even manage repairs. They also help ensure the property is always legally let by reminding you about inspection dates and when safety certificates need renewing. Tools like these are designed to make your work more professional and reduce the chance of you missing something important.

For property maintenance and repairs, you need to seek out reliable contractors - builders, plumbers, electricians and cleaners - that you know will respond quickly and help you deal with issues before they become major problems.

Have an inspection schedule and a list of things to check, inside and outside the property, and make sure you set aside money each month – not only for ongoing general maintenance but also to cover any sudden repairs.

When it comes to tenant communication, it's well worth while setting up a dedicated email address or message app to make it easier to track and record issues, complaints and disputes. Keep all messages polite and professional and if there's a problem, respond quickly and clearly so that tenants feel heard and respected. Remember, managing people well is just as important as managing a property.

I'd also recommend joining the National Residential Landlords Association (NRLA), which provides practical resources, legal support and access to a huge range of training courses to help you be a professional landlord. You also get discounts on all kinds of products and services, which should more than cover the membership fee.

Lastly, make sure you have a reliable way of keeping up to date with landlord regulation. The NRLA will keep you informed, but it's also worth signing up for newsletters from platforms like LandlordZONE (landlordzone.co.uk) and joining local property groups and landlord associations to make sure you don't miss out on any changes to the rules in your specific area.

Stevenage

HMO LETTINGS ™

Local Experts in
HMO Property management

Chapter Summary

There's a lot of work involved in running an HMO, and it's not something you should take on yourself unless you're confident you've got the time, knowledge and skills to deal effectively with the many different aspects of the business, which include:

- ✓ Legal compliance
- ✓ Marketing and selling rooms
- ✓ Building good relationships with tenants, contractors and suppliers
- ✓ Scheduling and tracking maintenance
- ✓ Organising repairs
- ✓ Receiving and handling complaints
- ✓ Mediating and helping resolve disputes
- ✓ Keeping detailed records

If you're happy with all that, self-management gives you much greater control over your investment, will help maximise your profits and can also be very personally rewarding – that's why so many HMO landlords have built portfolios.

Conversely, putting your property in the hands of a Propertymark member letting agent could be a very convenient option. They can ensure your property and tenants are managed professionally and take on much of the responsibility for legal compliance, saving you a huge amount of time, effort and worry.

While there's a significant cost to using an agent, remember to put a value on your own time. That's not just the actual time it takes to complete tasks, but also the time you have to spend thinking about the property. Divide the agent's fee by those hours – is that an hourly rate you're happy with, or would it actually be more cost-effective to outsource?

If you'd really like to self-manage but have doubts about whether you can handle everything, remember that you can almost always do more than you think!

It's perfectly natural to be nervous about taking on something new, but if you've been involved in operating any aspect of a business, have experience of managing people, already run your own household, and you're ready and willing to learn, you should be able to run an HMO.

Just make sure you have the right support. Join a landlord association, network with other local investors, get some decent contractors on your side – and keep this book to hand!

Chapter Eleven

Scaling Up Your HMO Strategy

Once your first HMO is up and running and you've gained some experience of the whole process – and especially when you see the rent rolling in each month! – if you're anything like me, you'll be thinking about the next one. Expanding your property portfolio will increase your income, give you more appreciating assets, and put you on the path to turning property into a full-time business (if that's what you want).

But scaling up comes with new challenges. Financing is likely to require more creative thinking and, if you're not outsourcing to an agent, managing multiple properties means you need to focus more on building the right team around you.

A successful HMO portfolio strategy is about far more than just doing the same thing over and over. You need a carefully thought-out plan that will enable you to grow without becoming overwhelmed. That includes understanding your cash flow, using the right legal structures, and knowing when to delegate. Whether you want to own two properties or twenty, you've got to scale in a way that keeps your properties profitable, your tenants happy, and your stress levels low.

Before making any moves towards buying a second property, review how your first HMO is performing. Is it making a healthy profit? Are your management and admin systems running smoothly? Are your tenants happy? Most importantly, are you enjoying being a landlord? If the answer is yes, you're ready for the next step.

Next, what kind of property do you want to buy? If you went for something that just needed a minor refurb the first time around, would you rather do the same again, or are you up for a bigger challenge? If you don't have access to a lot of capital at the moment, maybe you'd prefer to buy an existing HMO that shouldn't need any money spending on it for a couple of years. (You might want to take another look at Chapter Four...)

In reality, your first HMO will probably have been a big experiment for you, and a huge learning curve, and that's going to play into your decision about your next move. No matter how much research you did in the beginning and how many experienced landlords you took advice from, it's only once you've gained first-hand experience that you really understand what works and what doesn't, and can see little changes that you could make to improve your profitability and how you run your property business.

My point here is, if your first investment wasn't quite as great as you hoped or thought it would be, don't worry – that's completely normal! As I said in Chapter Two, as long as it was a good deal and it's turning a decent enough profit, tick it off and move on. This next purchase is your opportunity to put what you've learned into practice and have some healthy competition with yourself to make number two an even better rental property.

Importantly, just because you've done it successfully once, don't think you can cut corners second time around. Even if you're aiming to buy a similar property in the same area, go back and do all the research again. Markets can change, demand can shift, and tenants' expectations seem to grow every year! And if you want to branch out into a different area, don't assume that what worked in one location will necessarily work somewhere else - be prepared to adapt to the specific demand.

Run the numbers thoroughly. The good news is, this should be quicker and easier than last time, because you'll understand exactly what you need to do and will have the spreadsheets all set up to calculate your KPIs.

Finally, think about your systems, processes and record-keeping. The bigger your business grows, the more organised you need to be, and as you go along, you'll probably need to invest some time and money in new tools and better communication systems. You'll certainly need to invest in education and be willing to keep learning.

Landlords who have been there and done it are one of your most valuable resources, so don't hesitate to seek help and advice along the way. One of the things I now get the most pleasure and satisfaction from is sharing my knowledge and experience, both by mentoring newer HMO landlords and chewing things over with my peers in the business. Even after 35 years in the property world, I still don't know everything!

Leveraging Financing Options

One of the biggest challenges of scaling your HMO business is finding the money to buy more properties. Luckily, there are several different financing strategies and options out there that can help you grow, including HMO mortgages, releasing equity, commercial finance, bridging loans and private investment partners. Once you understand these tools, you can choose the best one for your circumstances and goals.

The most common choice, especially for new landlords, is an HMO mortgage. These loans are a niche within the buy-to-let market, specifically designed for landlords of multi-let properties. Because they're seen as higher risk than traditional BTL homes, they tend to come with higher interest rates than some regular BTL mortgages, and the criteria for HMO mortgages are tighter, with lenders treating it more like a business loan than a mortgage.

There are limits on how many HMOs one lender will finance, and many lenders limit the number of properties you can own in one area, plus, once you have existing HMOs, they'll want to see that they're performing well before giving you another loan.

Bridging loans are short-term loans used to buy or renovate a property quickly. They're an expensive way of borrowing but can be useful when speed matters. For example, you might use a bridging loan to buy a run-down house, renovate it into an HMO, and then refinance with a longer-term mortgage once it's ready. This is known as "buy, refurbish, refinance" (BRR).

Another powerful tool is using private finance or joint ventures, where you partner up with someone who has money to invest but doesn't want to manage property and is simply looking for decent returns. This approach can help you scale faster without using all your own money. You can structure the agreement in whatever way suits you, but essentially they fund the deal, you do the work, and you split the profits.

You might pay them a monthly return out of the profits, agree a specific equity split, or a combination of the two. Two important things to know:

1. With any joint venture, you need a watertight side legal agreement that reflects each party's financial interest and sets out clear terms.
2. If you require a mortgage and someone else is funding or part-funding the deposit, they legally have to be on the mortgage and the ownership of the property. If they're putting up the whole deposit, the lender could require them to take out the mortgage in their name.

Refinancing to Release Equity and Boost your ROI

Having a mortgage in property investment is a great idea, especially when it comes to a high-income HMO strategy that gives you plenty of rental income to fund the repayments. When the property goes up in value, all the equity is yours (less tax, of course) – you benefit from the growth on both your own invested funds *and* the bank's money!

Over time, as your properties increase in value, you should have the option of remortgaging and releasing some of the equity growth. And the less of your own money you have tied up in a property, the greater your ROI will be. As I said earlier, if you can get your head around "good" debt – debt that doesn't cost you personally anything to service – you can get to the point where your business is funded entirely by the bank, giving you an infinite ROI.

This is how you do it:

Let's say that after 3 years, your £300,000 HMO purchase from Chapter Three (bought with a 25% deposit) is now worth £388,000*, so your £75,000 equity has grown to £163,000. If you can remortgage at 75% LTV (loan to value), that means you need to leave £97,000 equity in the property (25% 'deposit') but can release up to £66,000 - and that could be enough to fund the deposit for another property.

**At the time of writing, Savills / Oxford Economics is forecasting 16% average house price growth between the start of 2026 and the end of*

2028, and factoring in the capital increase forced by the refurb, I would say a 30% uplift over 3 years should be achievable.

Now you've brought down the amount of your own capital tied up in the investment from £115,000 (£75,000 deposit plus £40,000 costs) to £49,000. Given that you should be able to increase rents at above the rate of inflation, we'll assume your rental profits have risen slightly to £22,000.

Your ROI has now gone from 17.4% to almost 45% in just three years.
(£22,000 ÷ £49,000) x 100

Of course, that's a simplistic example – for instance, your mortgage repayments may have increased, but you get the idea. And if you recycle your capital by using the equity you released to buy another HMO, your money is now working harder for you. The capital that was tied up in one property, generating £1,500 - £2,000 monthly profit, is now split between two properties, generating £3,000 - £4,000. You've probably had to inject some more money on top of the equity, but you've still significantly increased your ROI.

I know investors who have been in the business for longer than me, who have some investments that don't owe them anything. All the equity in their properties is growth, and they've been able to release all their invested capital over time. Their mortgage costs are higher than they used to be because they've borrowed more, but their profits provide an infinite ROI because the business is funded by the bank's money and rental income.

CAVEAT: Always leave enough equity in the property to cover the capital gains bill and disposal costs.

Capital gains tax becomes due at the point you sell or transfer ownership of the property, and it's based on the difference between the purchase price and the value at the time of disposal – not the equity you're left with! So you've got to keep an eye on how much you'd owe the tax man if you had to sell tomorrow and make sure the equity in the property will cover it.

For instance, you buy a property for £250,000 and hold it for 15 years. During that time, you periodically refinance at 75% LTV. At the point you sell, it's worth £400,000 and your 25% equity is £100,000. However, that's not what you walk away with.

The capital gain is £150,000. If we apply the current tax-free allowance of £3,000 and the CGT higher rate of 24%, that's a bill of £35,280, leaving you with £64,720 (less the selling agent's fee and other disposal costs).

If you think that's not very much of a lump sum to walk away with at the end of a 15-year property investment, remember you've been benefitting from great month-on-month profits. And if you've managed to release most of the capital you invested over time, then the property really doesn't owe you anything!

Take Specialist Professional Advice

These aren't decisions you should be making on your own, no matter how much research you've done. Investment property ownership and taxation are pretty complex, and I'd go so far as to say you'd be extremely foolish to make any decisions without consulting a legal property expert, a property tax specialist, a wealth manager and a buy to let specialist broker – ideally professionals who invest in property themselves.

And when you speak to these people, go with a business plan. It doesn't have to be detailed but you should have some idea of how you want things to pan out, including:

- What other income and assets do you have that contribute to your overall wealth and how might that change going forward? (Inheritance, work bonuses, other investments maturing...)
- Roughly how many properties do you expect/want to own?
- What kind of returns do you need (ongoing income & capital lump sums) and when?
- What are your future plans for passing on or selling these properties, and have you thought about inheritance and Trust planning? (See the next chapter.)

Of course, you'll have to pay for the best advice, but in my experience it's 100% worth the up-front investment. It'll pay you back many times over what you spend, in tax savings and overall profitability. And the consequences of not consulting with these experts and getting the structure of your business and financing wrong could have a disastrous impact – some decisions are very hard or even impossible to remedy after the fact.

Building a Team for Growth

As your HMO business grows, you won't be able to do everything yourself. Managing more properties means more tenants, more responsibility, more admin – more work in general. That's why it's essential to build a reliable team that can take the day-to-day business off your hands so that you can focus on the bigger picture.

Think of your team as the engine that powers your growth.

This is about building a property management team, on top of your team of professional advisers (accountant, legal company, mortgage adviser, surveyor, etc.). It's a combination of staff and service providers that might ultimately include:

- Property manager
- Lettings assistant
- Bookkeeper
- Cleaners
- Gardeners
- General building contractors
- 'Handyman'

Each person should be skilled, trustworthy, and clear about their role. Start by approaching people you've worked with before and trust. If you're new to an area, ask other landlords for recommendations and certainly don't just pick the cheapest option – that rarely ends well!

Communication is key. Make sure everyone on your team knows your expectations and set clear timelines for things like repairs, legal deadlines, and rent collection. When everyone knows what's happening, problems are less likely to occur, so use shared calendars or apps to stay organised.

There's always a sticky period when you've got maybe two or three properties and it's a bit too much work for you to handle yourself, but you don't feel you can afford to employ someone or find office space. A good solution can be to hire a virtual assistant or part-time administrator, who can help with emails, rent reminders, paperwork and tenant queries.

The other challenge can simply be letting go and delegating, particularly if you're something of a perfectionist and/or you've taken a lot of pride in providing an excellent home and management service to your tenants thus far.

The reality is that it's incredibly hard to find employees that care as much about the details as you. Great people are out there and sometimes you find a real gem, someone who's perfectly suited to a particular job. But be prepared for the fact that you may need to compromise a little, and that's just something you've got to deal with, because as you grow, you can't possibly do everything yourself.

Photo by Major Tom Agency on Unsplash

It's about finding a team that can get tasks done, hit the important deadlines and metrics, and that you trust. Will everything be done 100% as you'd ideally like? Probably not. But you need to let them get on with it so that you can spend your time driving the business forward - finding new property deals and ways of improving existing returns. Delegating doesn't mean losing control—it means running your business like a professional.

Chapter Summary

Scaling up your HMO strategy involves more than just buying more houses. It's about expanding your portfolio wisely, using smart and appropriate financing options, and building a strong, reliable team to support your business.

Throughout your expansion, always keep a close eye on your overall financial health. Monitoring the performance and cashflow of your HMOs is one side of the business (Chapter Three), but your own financial profile needs to be healthy in order for you to keep securing funding.

Lenders look at your income, credit score and existing debts, and a strong financial profile opens doors to better deals. So, before applying for new loans, reduce any unnecessary spending and make sure all your financial records are up to date. And check in regularly with your various financial and mortgage advisers to make sure you remain in the best possible position to keep growing.

Each step forward requires planning, patience, and the willingness to adapt, but when it's done well, scaling up can increase your returns while reducing your personal workload, and enable you to turn a property sideline into a stable, long-term business.

Chapter Twelve

Planning for the Future

When you start your journey as an HMO investor, it's easy to focus only on the next deal. But true success in property investment comes from thinking long-term and planning for the future. What will your portfolio look like and how will it be performing in five, ten and even twenty years? How will your goals change over that time and where do you envisage your investment journey ending?

You might be in the prime of your life right now, but if you want to get the best out of your business in the future, you need to think right into your retirement, and about what will happen when you decide to slow down, step back or sell.

The property market is always changing, with new rules, technology, and trends. You've got to stay informed and be ready to adjust your strategy as necessary to keep realising great returns. Some changes may be good, like new areas growing in demand for HMOs. Others may be tough, such as tax changes or rising costs. With the right mindset, you can make smart choices that protect your income and build long-term value.

In this chapter, we'll look at three important topics: planning your exit or retirement, adapting to changes in the property market, and keeping your HMO business profitable for years to come.

Exit Strategies and Retirement Planning

How you structure the financing and legal ownership of your properties from the word go will impact the returns your portfolio delivers to you and/or your beneficiaries in the future. So, whether you want to retire early or pass your properties on to your children, you can't afford to underestimate the importance of taking specialist legal, tax and wealth management advice from the very start.

To get the best advice, you need to know where you're going and that means having a clear idea of your whole investment journey, including an exit plan. The earlier you start planning, the more options you'll have available to you and the less likely you are to come up against any nasty surprises, like an unexpected capital gains tax bill for you or your children.

Think about what kind of lifestyle you want in the future and whether ongoing income or lump sum returns would be more useful to you in satisfying your goals. Do you want to give up work and travel, simply be able to enjoy a decent passive income, or maybe buy the luxury home or yacht of your dreams?! Would you like to pay for your grandchildren's education or give your own children a secure future?

Perhaps your goal is to build up sufficient funds through property to invest in another business that will invigorate a local community. Maybe you want to be a benefactor to a charity or set up a foundation. Perhaps you'd like to do a combination of all these things....whatever you want your future to look like, having clear personal goals will shape your property plans.

If your intention is to sell your properties to realise the capital profits, it's usually more financially beneficial and tax-efficient to do that gradually, selling one at a time over a number of years. Obviously, the bigger your portfolio, the longer that will take, so you need to think about a rough schedule – and appreciate it may have to change depending on the market at the time.

Another option is to keep some, if not all of the properties and live off the rental income into your retirement, then eventually pass them on to family or loved ones. This takes careful planning, especially when it comes to taxes, and the earlier you can make a sound Will and put in place things like a trust or limited company share structure, the better.

Because of the complexities of gifting or Willing property, it's essential you find the very best specialists to help put the right legal and financial structures in place.

Without wishing to sound morbid, none of us knows what's round the corner, so it's well worth speaking to an estate planner sooner rather than later and making sure your legal representative and financial adviser or wealth manager have your written permission to speak to each other.

It's never too early to start these conversations. Having a clear exit plan will make your whole investment journey smoother, more rewarding and more profitable.

Adapting to Market Trends

The property market moves in cycles. Although the rental market is much more stable than the sales market – mainly because rents move in line with wages – supply and demand can and do fluctuate, laws change, and tenant needs evolve.

As an HMO landlord, staying up to date is vital if you want to maintain full occupancy and avoid any legal pitfalls. Ignoring trends can lead to a drop in your income, but if you're flexible and can adapt early to new opportunities, you should be able to sustain strong returns.

One big trend is the demand for better quality rooms. Tenants expect more than just a bed and four walls. They want fast internet, environmentally friendly amenities, clean shared spaces, and a good service, so you've got to be prepared to invest in keeping your property modern and well-maintained.

Look for the little things that will make it stand out from the competition. Even small upgrades like better lighting and smart locks can make a big difference and attract better tenants. As younger renters move into the market, they expect convenience, and tech is at the forefront of their lives, so you need to know what's out there and adopt the products and tools that make sense. From keyless entry to online payments and virtual viewings, tech can save time and improve tenant satisfaction.

When it comes to the environment and particularly energy standards, the government has been changing its mind on minimum requirements for years now. There's no doubt that in the future, rental properties will need to achieve higher than then current 'E' minimum EPC rating, but when that might come into effect – and how much notice we'll get - is unclear.

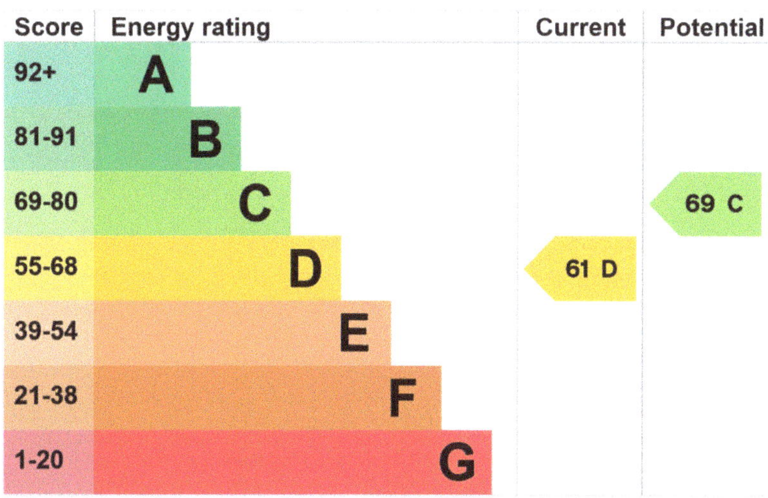

My advice is to do what you can at the point you renovate to "future proof" your HMO by making it as energy efficient as possible. That might mean adding insulation, changing windows, or switching to electric heating. While there's a cost, you need to be compliant and the "greener" your property, the more attractive it's likely to be to tenants. Energy efficiency isn't just good for the planet—it's good for business.

Finally, keep learning. Follow property news, attend landlord events and join local groups. The more informed you are, the easier it is to react to changes. Successful landlords see change as a chance to grow and improve, so stay curious and your business should stay strong.

Sustaining Long-Term Profitability

Cashflow and is what keeps your HMO business running and long-term profits come from consistency, planning, and smart decisions. To remain successful, you've got to keep costs under control, protect your income, and think ahead.

Start with regular maintenance and fixing issues as soon as you become aware of them. A well-maintained property keeps tenants happy, reducing the likelihood of complaints, and helps protect the capital value. Set a yearly budget for small repairs and keep track of wear and tear so you can adjust it if necessary. Importantly, factor in the cost of larger periodical repairs and upgrades and make sure you build up a reserve fund that will cover the cost when needed.

Next, review your rents every year. You need to stay competitive within your area, but if you don't increase rents by enough to at least keep up with inflation, the value of your profits drops. That's just one reason why you need to keep your property up to date and well-presented – so you can confidently charge a rate that's at the top of the local market, and tenants will still be keen to live in one of your rooms versus with a cheaper competitor.

Keep an eye on your mortgage and any other financing. Most lenders review their interest rates and deals every three months, and while you don't generally want to incur any early redemption penalties if you're on a fixed product, sometimes it can be worth the cost if you can make enough savings over time by switching. Find a good broker who specialises in HMO mortgages, and they should let you know when it might be worth moving. Reducing your monthly mortgage cost, even by a small amount, can boost your profits without any need to raise rent or cut maintenance or management costs.

Finally, review your figures and KPIs every three to six months, to make sure you're still on track, and see whether you can make any tweaks to improve your cashflow. That might be changing suppliers or simply renegotiating rates for services. And on an annual basis, check if there are any upgrades it might be worth investing in that would boost the market value of the property and/or enable you to charge a little more rent.

Long-term profit isn't about big leaps - it's about steady, smart steps over time.

Chapter Summary

A strong future is built on the decisions you make today, and planning for the future is a vital part of running a successful HMO business.

Whether it's preparing for retirement, adapting to market changes, or making sure you maintain your profits, thinking ahead gives you greater control and peace of mind. By putting an exit strategy in place early, you can enjoy the rewards of your hard work and make sure your efforts benefit you and your family for years to come.

Some Final Hints and Tips

Running an HMO business can feel like juggling a hundred things at once and as though there's a huge mountain to climb, especially when you're starting out. The good news is, now that the HMO market is well established, you don't have to make the same mistakes as landlords who have gone before you.

This chapter shares expert advice from seasoned investors, shows you how to avoid common problems, and gives you some quick wins that you can use straight away. Think of it like your cheat sheet for HMO success. From lessons learned through trial and error to smart habits that save time and money, these tips can help you make better decisions and grow with confidence.

Expert Advice from Seasoned Investors

One of the best ways to get ahead is to learn from people who've already been where you're going. Here are five expert tips that come up again and again from those who've built successful HMO portfolios:

1. **Start with a clear plan** – don't ever just buy a property and hope for the best! Know what kind of returns you're looking for, what type of tenants you want and what area will fit your goals. Having a well-thought-through plan will make every decision easier - from choosing a house to setting the rent.
2. **Run the numbers two or three times** to make sure your investment stacks up financially. Include not just your mortgage and bills, but also maintenance, insurance, void periods, and management costs. And "stress test" the figures to find out where your break-even point is and check you have enough of a financial buffer to ride out any likely storm without having to sell. It's far better to be realistic and cautious than to wing it and be caught off guard later.
3. **Keep it professional** and treat your HMO as you would any other business. Use proper systems and processes for rent collection, inspections, maintenance, and communication with tenants. You can be friendly and approachable without being casual. The more professional you are, the smoother you'll find things run.
4. **Invest in good tradespeople.** You need plumbers, electricians, builders and handymen that will respond to you quickly and do a good job. Build relationships with people you trust, pay a fair rate and settle invoices quickly. A reliable person you can call on when something goes wrong is worth their weight in gold.
5. **Never stop learning.** Markets shift, laws change, and tenant expectations grow. Read property news, join landlord forums, speak to other investors and make

sure you freely share your own knowledge and expertise – it's a two-way street.

Avoiding Common Pitfalls

Forewarned is forearmed! Here are five of the most common traps that many new landlords fall into – watch out for them and save yourself a lot of time, money, and stress:

- **Rushing into the wrong deal.** It's easy to get excited about your first property but buying without proper checks will almost certainly lead to big problems, either down the line or even as soon as you begin a refurb. Always research the area carefully, make sure the layout is right for an HMO, check local licensing policies, get a full survey and take advice from a builder or architect before moving ahead with a purchase.
- **Underestimating costs.** Many landlords forget about licensing fees, furniture, emergency repairs, voids and planning for future property works. Have a clear budget and set aside funds for future upgrades and repairs.
- **Poor tenant selection.** Don't skip background checks just to fill a room quickly. A bad tenant might cause trouble, stop paying rent or damage your property and you could have a long battle to get rid of them if they dig their heels in. Always vet them properly and trust your gut.

- **Falling foul of rules and regulations.** HMO laws are stricter than for standard BTL rentals and the penalties for breaching them can be severe. Ignoring or failing to find out about your obligations is no excuse - councils don't accept "I didn't know." So take the time and get professional advice to make sure your property meets fire safety rules, licensing rules, and health and safety standards.
- **Doing everything yourself.** Trying to save money by handling everything yourself can lead to stress and burnout. If you're managing more than one property, consider using a letting agent or virtual assistant for help. Delegating smartly isn't weakness - it's wisdom.

Quick Wins for New Investors

When you're just starting out, it helps to know about things you can do right away that won't cost a huge amount but can make a big difference. These five simple actions can improve your property, boost your rent and save you headaches from the start:

1. **Fresh paint and clean spaces.** A simple, fresh coat of paint and a deep clean make a huge impact. First impressions matter, and a bright, tidy home attracts better tenants and helps you stand out from the crowd, so always have a handyman refresh rooms between lets and keep your communal spaces up to spec.

2. **Provide fast Wi-Fi.** Internet is one of the top things tenants cares about. Investing in a good router and strong connection keeps everyone happy and helps your reviews. Make sure your provider knows how many people will be using the internet at the same time and can deliver a reliable service.
3. **Use key safes and smart locks.** Lost keys and locked doors can be a hassle. A coded key safe or smart lock means tenants can get in easily, and you can manage access without running across town every time someone forgets their key.
4. **Set clear house rules.** Write down simple, fair rules for things like cleaning, noise, and guests. It avoids conflict later and makes expectations clear from day one. A happy house is a house with clear communication.
5. **Use management apps.** There are apps and software for pretty much every aspect of being a landlord, including tracking rent, handling repairs and organising documents. These save time and keep everything in one place.

Tools for Smarter Investing

Head to **www.richardleonardhmoexpert.co.uk** to download two essential tools to help you avoid costly mistakes and give you more confidence when embarking on a new HMO investment:

- Return on Investment (ROI) calculator to help you measure whether a deal stacks up and makes financial sense
- Property Research Checklist to guide you through researching a property, area, and the local rules

Whether you're looking at your first deal or your tenth, these templates will guide you through the basics of financial planning and property research. They don't require fancy maths skills—just a little focus and a willingness to use all available data.

In Conclusion…

I hope you've found this book genuinely interesting, enlightening and useful, and that you're now all pumped up and inspired to get out there and find your first (or next) HMO project!

When I started out, although I had some great fellow investors and mentors I could learn from and lean on, I didn't have a resource that spelt everything out as clearly as I've tried to do here. That's why I wrote this book – it's me giving something back to the next generation of professional HMO landlords that will take the market forward in the coming decades.

So, now that you're hopefully several steps closer to success, I look forward to welcoming you to the growing community I'm so proud to be a part of.

HMO
Property Sourcing

www.hmopropertysourcing.co.uk

www.stevenagelettings.com

Let me help you on your property journey!

Writing HMO Expert has been a true pleasure — a chance to share the insights, lessons, and systems that have helped me and many others succeed in the world of HMO investing.

Over the years, I've had the privilege of guiding both beginners and seasoned investors to achieve consistent results and confidence in their HMO ventures.

Whether you're just starting out or scaling up, I'm here to help. So if you're looking for practical advice, one-to-one support - or even if you just fancy a chat about HMOs - reach out any time:

info@richardleonardhmoexpert.co.uk

Let's make your next investment your best one!

About the Author

Richard Leonard is a successful property investor, author, mentor and property coach with over 30 years' experience in the property industry. He is the proud owner of a high income-generating HMO portfolio currently worth around £5 million.

Before becoming a full-time property investor, Richard built a solid career in consultancy and technology project management, delivering complex and demanding solutions to a number of large corporate clients, including BT, Cable & Wireless, National Grid, Barclays and Coca-Cola.

Richard also founded Lenwell Property Management in 1990, which has helped manage and develop housing across the South-East of England. His background has given him a deep understanding of building processes, planning and smart investing, and his full membership of the Association for Project Management (MAPM) demonstrates his professional credibility in managing complex projects from start to finish.

To date, he has successfully raised £2.8 million in investor capital, which he has used in the acquisition and development of 18 high-quality HMOs. These projects have provided secure, modern housing for hundreds of tenants, while giving strong returns to his investors.

He published his first book, 'HMO Renovation & Refurbishment Success', to help other landlords learn how to renovate and upgrade properties with confidence. That book focused on the building side of HMO investing; this one covers the whole HMO landlord journey, from research and acquisition, through managing properties and tenancies, to scaling a portfolio and planning for the future.

Richard lives in East Hertfordshire, with his family. He's passionate about his family and friends and motorcycling, and he's also an avid Chelsea supporter.

Also available on Amazon:

Testimonials

I've had the pleasure of knowing Richard for over three years now, both as a friend and a fellow property investment coach. Working alongside him has been not only inspiring but also a lot of fun. Richard brings a rare blend of professionalism, warmth, and wit to everything he does — especially when we're presenting together.

HMO Expert is the culmination of Richard's 25 years of hands-on experience in property investing. His depth of knowledge, paired with a genuine passion for helping others succeed, shines through on every page. Whether you're just starting out or looking to fine-tune your strategy, this book is full of practical wisdom and golden nuggets to help you build a thriving HMO property portfolio. A must-read for anyone serious about taking their property journey to the next level.
Abi Hookway, Property Investment Coach

Richard came to me for mentoring after decades as an investor, because he understands that mastery is a constant journey, not a one-time event. It also shows his humility, which is rare in someone with his level of experience. He is a caring person with unparalleled expertise in the world of HMOs, and it has been a real pleasure to mentor him and now call him a friend.

His depth of knowledge in HMOs is rare, and he genuinely cares about creating great homes for tenants while running profitable investments. If you want to succeed in property investment, read his book. It is packed with practical, real-world insights from someone who has truly walked the walk.
Steve Doran, Property Coach

I first met Richard when we both worked for a large corporate in the City of London. In our spare time we were both dabbling in single property rentals. Richard spent some time researching HMOs as an option and entered the market. After a few months we did a careful evaluation of Richard's progress, and my wife and I decided to follow Richard's lead.

He helped us to locate suitable properties in areas of good demand with reasonable rental returns. Using his team of sub-contractors, he managed the refurbishment of each property, providing a full turnkey solution.

His Letting and Management Agency then sourced our tenants and took on the management of the property. This arrangement has now been in place for over 10 years, and we couldn't be more pleased. It has allowed my wife and I to retire with an extra monthly income, which we never would have envisaged had I not met Richard.

Richard is a dedicated individual who has a real passion for property. He is also a thoroughly nice guy!
Dave Fox

"Over the years Richard has impressed me not only as an expert property investor but even more so as a father. What he did by building his HMO portfolio enabled him to quit work and spend the time and (a lot of) money to care for one of his children who needed brain cancer treatment in the USA.

Most people could not have done that: Richard built a life that meant he was handsomely rewarded for not working. Let that sink in. Now decide if you want to do the same thing.

If your answer is yes, then Richard Leonard is the person to listen to about HMOs. Enjoy the book and the rewards of your HMO journey.
Paul Smith BSc (Hons) MBA, Founder of Touchstone Education

Rich and I go way back — almost 20 years — to our days in the corporate world at Eversheds. Over time, we became close friends, supporting each other as we branched out to form our own businesses. That journey created a long-distance sounding board for both of us, a trusted connection we've continued to rely on through the years.

While I built a large procurement practice, Richard steadily grew his property portfolio. He'd often have me in stitches with stories about tenants, property deals, and the many ups and downs that came with them. In turn, I'd share my own challenges — dealing with tricky clients or needing his insight on a business problem. We've always had each other's backs.

What I truly admire about Richard is how he's turned a genuine passion for property into a thriving business that he truly enjoys. And when I say passion, I mean *real* passion — he lives and breathes it. What's more, he loves helping aspiring property investors and giving back through his knowledge. That just shows how deeply he cares about people's success.

Well done, Rich — truly inspirational.
Jenny Powell

I'm not in the HMO game, but as a human being, family man, best friend and "wingman", I can certainly say that Richard is an unstoppable force of positive energy, ideas and support. It is no surprise to anyone that knows him that he has made this dream a reality.
Colin Hoffmeister

I've had the privilege of knowing and working alongside Richard Leonard for 15 years, both as a trusted friend and a respected colleague within the UK HMO property industry. Throughout our journey, I've witnessed firsthand Richard's unwavering commitment to excellence, his deep industry knowledge, and his ability to adapt and innovate in an ever-evolving market.

What sets Richard apart is not just his expertise, but his integrity, generosity, and genuine desire to see others succeed. Whether he's structuring complex deals, mentoring new investors, or navigating regulatory challenges, Richard brings a level of clarity and confidence that makes a lasting impact.

His new book, HMO Expert, is a true reflection of the passion and professionalism Richard brings to everything he does. It's not only an insightful guide for anyone in or entering the HMO space, but also a testament to the values he lives by. I couldn't be prouder to endorse his work, and I know readers will walk away informed, inspired, and ready to take action.
Nick Fox, HMO Property Investor, Author of HMO Property Success

Would you like to be a published author?

Of course you would! What better way to support your marketing efforts and enhance your reputation?

Since 2008, I've worked with a variety of entrepreneurs, ghostwriting or editing books and guiding them through the self-publishing process.

To find out more about how I can help you produce a 'thick business card' that perfectly showcases your knowledge and expertise, visit:

www.thickbusinesscard.co.uk

Sarah Walker
Freelance Writer & Editor

www.ingramcontent.com/pod-product-compliance
Lightning Source LLC
LaVergne TN
LVHW050912210926
848482LV00012B/413
9781919373102